THE SELF-TALK SOLUTION

Shad Helmstetter

POCKET BOOKS
New York   London   Toronto   Sydney   Tokyo   Singapore

POCKET BOOKS, a division of Simon & Schuster Inc.
1230 Avenue of the Americas, New York, NY 10020

Copyright © 1987 by Shad Helmstetter
Self-Talk scripts from Part II of *The Self-Talk Solution*
copyright © 1982, 1983, 1984, 1985, 1986, 1987.

ISBN: 0-671-72757-5

First Pocket Books printing October 1988

10 9 8 7 6 5 4

POCKET and colophon are registered trademarks of
Simon & Schuster Inc.

Printed in the U.S.A.

THE SELF-TALK SOLUTION

can help you reprogram your mind to accomplish *permanent behavioral change*. Recent scientific discoveries have shown that what we think and say can cause physical and bio-chemical changes in the body. Let Dr. Shad Helmstetter show you how positive Self-Talk can transform your mind, your body and your life!

Self-Talk for Money Management

"I just can't seem to get ahead"; "I spend more than I make" . . . This kind of self-talk *guarantees* money *mis*-management. Here is a better kind of Self-Talk that will help you see yourself as a better money manager:

- I am consciously aware of every dollar I spend, and where I spend it.

- Because I manage money well, I am always able to save some of what I earn. I set monthly and yearly savings goals and I meet them . . .

Self-Talk for Exercising

"I get started but I just can't stay with it"; "I would love to exercise more if I had the time" . . . There is a better way to coach yourself. The Self-Talk in this script will help you get in shape *and stay with it:*

- I really like being in good shape! I take care of myself and I keep myself fit.

- When I set a goal, I reach it. I stay with it, and nothing can stop me!

- I'm a great coach! I keep myself up, motivated, enthusiastic, and going for it . . .

And *Much* More!

Books by Shad Helmstetter

Choices
Finding the Fountain of Youth Inside Yourself
Predictive Parenting: What to Say When You Talk to
  Your Kids
The Self-Talk Solution
What to Say When You Talk to Yourself
You Can Excel in Times of Change

Published by POCKET BOOKS

*This book is dedicated to my nephew
André Helmstetter, who first asked me,
many years ago, that profound question:
"Why are some people successful
and some people are not?"*

A·C·K·N·O·W·L·E·D·G·M·E·N·T·S

There are many who have helped along the way. I would especially like to thank Holly Hill, Re'Ann Brown, and Don and Julia Hays who continue to question, enlighten, and enhance any thought I had that I thought was my own; Bill Adler, one of the most remarkable literary individuals of our time; and my exceptionally skilled and understanding editor, Adrian Zackheim. I owe a special debt of gratitude to Kathryn Sorensen, the first teacher who courageously took Self-Talk into dozens of grade-school classrooms. In addition to the many others who have made this book possible, I would especially like to thank the tireless researchers who have begun to unlock the secrets of the human brain. It is through their efforts that we have started to unlock a few of the secrets of what we call the "mind." And I also would like to thank my son Gregory, who plays his quieter, most inspirational piano compositions when he knows I have a deadline to meet, and I am trying to write.

C·O·N·T·E·N·T·S

P · A · R · T **II**
THE WORDS OF SELF-TALK

I·N·T·R·O·D·U·C·T·I·O·N

This is a book that refused to wait any longer to be written. Several years before I wrote *What to Say When You Talk to Your Self,* I had compiled and edited a collection of the words and phrases of Self-Talk. At the time, I considered putting all of the best Self-Talk together in one easy-reading reference guide. But Self-Talk proved to have a mind of its own; it was not to be caged so easily.

In a few short years I was to see Self-Talk grow from a simple concept, practiced by a few self-motivated individuals, to a phenomenon that encompassed virtually every segment of the population. During that time the words, phrases, and scripts of Self-Talk, many of which appear in this book, have been put into practice by literally tens of thousands of individuals.

Where once only a handful of individuals took Self-Talk to heart, the new down-to-earth techniques of self-direction soon caught the attention of others who had been disappointed with motivational theories that had failed to live up to their promises. Self-Talk began to appear in corporate offices, churches, backyards, and grade-school classrooms. The word spread fast. Within a few months of the publication of *What to Say When You Talk to Your Self,* people who had never before considered it possible to change how they think, were writing letters to the publisher asking for more. The first book opened the door for them. Now they were ready to get moving.

The letters I received were from a cross-section of our culture. I heard from business people, parents, clergymen, medical doctors, psychologists, psychiatrists, salespeople, teachers, students, grandparents, eight-year-olds, lifelong achievers, and first-time hopefuls. The stories of their successes would be an inspiration to anyone.

But although Self-Talk was being used successfully by people from different walks of life, many of them wrote to me because they wanted to learn additional techniques for putting Self-Talk into practice. And most of them wanted to learn more of the actual words—Self-Talk "scripts" that covered specific day-to-day situations—already written out and ready to use.

The new information, and the additional Self-Talk readers were asking for, surpassed the amount of material I had originally compiled for a short Self-Talk reference guide—then titled *The Complete Book of Self-Talk*. There was clearly more that needed to be said. There were newfound techniques that had come from the users themselves. There were real people in real situations who had learned to bring their personal Self-Talk to life in their own homes and jobs. There were suggestions for important new areas that could benefit from specially written Self-Talk scripts. And there were good questions that deserved good answers.

This book is the result. It presents the latest information in the significant new field of Self-Management. It gives you an inside view of the process and the effects of Self-Talk in the lives of people around you. And it offers you, the reader, the most comprehensive collection of practical, usable Self-Talk ever compiled in a single source.

This book has turned out to be more comprehensive than my original conception of the Self-Talk reference guide. That is due in part to a responsive public. But it is also the result of recognizing the need to allow something worthwhile to have its own way. Some things, when they are ready to be noticed, seem to have a way of being heard. Self-Talk—the management of your self by the direction of your own thoughts—is like that. It appears that its time has come.

WHAT IT IS AND HOW IT WORKS

ONE

THE TREASURE

When I was a young boy growing up in a small farm town in the Midwest, I had what would become one of my most unforgettable adventures. My hometown sat securely in the middle of an unending patchwork of fields of wheat and corn and soybeans and flax. The town itself measured only a mile in each direction and, according to the small sign at its edge, boasted a population of 2,500 friendly inhabitants. It had tree-lined streets, two schools, a dozen or so churches, and a wealth of opportunities for any young boy or girl, who had grown up on Hardy Boys mysteries, to create any imaginable adventure.

My adventure was the search for a treasure that we had good reason to believe actually existed. The small house my family and I lived in sat on the farthest edge of town. Across the cinder road that marked the perimeter of town was a grove of plum trees, and beyond that, as far as the eye could see, there was nothing but fields, dotted here and there with a stand of trees that guarded the barns and the home of the farmer who worked the surrounding fields.

A few blocks away, within sight of the safety of our home, was an old, deserted, and most certainly haunted house. Surrounded by thickets and sheds and stands of

3

gnarled old trees, it was the kind of place you would avoid on a windy moonless night when broken screen doors creaked on their hinges and branches tapped at dark, staring windows.

Even on the brightest day, that old house with its abandoned woodsheds, its unruly landscape of overgrown gardens and tall dark trees, conjured up visions of hidden secrets and buried treasures from the past. For highly imaginative adventurers, the old house and its surrounding grounds represented unending possibilities.

At the time it never occurred to us children that we might only be imagining most of what we believed about the old place. We weren't surprised when the old man arrived and began to thrash through the dilapidated old buildings as if he were looking for something.

He was an ornery old man. He didn't like kids, and he especially didn't like us when we followed him around, asking if we could help. The first day, when we saw him pulling loose boards from old woodshed walls and digging through the coarse dirt on the floors of the old outbuildings, we tried to make him our friend. But instead of talking to us, he gruffly pushed us aside, and went about his business of looking and digging and prodding and searching.

Since we were adventurous youngsters, it did not take us long to figure out that this old man was looking for something—and we suspected it just might be the treasure we had imagined finding all along. So we had a meeting and decided that we should do everything possible to make the old man our friend, and learn as much as we could about the treasure we were sure he was looking for.

The old man never really did warm up to us. But he did end up enlisting our help. He agreed to give each of us a nickel if we found something that looked like a box.

Earlier, on one of our more daring forays into the interior of the old house itself, we had found a yellowed scroll of paper, written in a language we could not read, hidden in the wall of an upstairs room. But now we kept even this to ourselves. We had learned from questioning our parents that the old man, in his seventies, was the son of the family that had emigrated to our town from Europe and had built the old house many years earlier. We had also been told that not only should we avoid the old man, but that we should not play on the property where he was spending his time each day.

The old man looked long and hard, but the only thing he ever found was an old purplish-colored, pocket-sized leather coin sack that contained nothing more than some rusted keys and a few old coins. This he had found between the wall-boards of one of the old sheds. Finally he went away, and we never saw him again.

But what fire his presence had added to our imagination! Now we *knew* that the old house *did* have a secret. The old man had given us more belief in our treasure than we could ever have created for ourselves. Now we were *sure* that the treasure existed. And now we could find it for ourselves.

And so we set out. We were not exactly the sort of group you would expect to find any treasure at all: My older sister, Carmel, who was thirteen, my eight-year-old brother Verne, a twelve-year-old neighbor girl named Rebecca, and I, twelve years old, made up the crew.

But we were inventive. We had noticed, in our search-ings with the old man, a peculiar grouping of large smooth stones in the middle of a small stand of trees. In that circle of trees was a large stone the size of a man's body, set below a single round stone, two straight, long stones extending down from the body stone, and one more long stone extending out from the others. Together, the five stones created the perfect image of a man lying down, torso, head, legs, and one arm— pointing very clearly in one direction. Those stones, we thought, were the clue. Their arrangement *must* give us a clear direction to the treasure.

If you plotted a line from the extended arm of the stone man, it pointed directly toward the center of three lone trees that stood in the shape of a triangle about twenty feet from the stone figure. *That point,* we reasoned, in the exact center of those three trees must be where the treasure was buried.

At this time in my life, as adventurous as my friends and I were, we had one mighty adversary. Once we had found the spot where we knew the treasure must be, we had to over-come only one obstacle—my father. He had decreed that *none* of us, *for any reason,* could play on the lot by the old house. Unfortunately, the area our father had placed off limits was the precise location of our buried treasure. If we were to dig it up and live a life of riches—which, as young folks, we totally believed we would—not only would we have to disobey a direct order from our father, we would also have to avoid getting caught digging a large hole on the property where we were not supposed to be in the first place.

Our solution, as it so often was in cases like that, was to do it anyway. One of us would stand guard, a lookout in the event the evil pirate—Father—showed up unexpectedly, and the rest of us would take turns digging. Looking back, I don't think that any of us really expected to find anything. But we wanted to believe. That is how young minds work.

We started early the next Saturday morning. We marked the spot, and we dug. I turned the first spade, and then with each shovelful began to dig with an increasing sense of urgency. What if, I thought, someone, especially our father, found out what we were doing? He wouldn't understand. And so we dug, and the first few shovelfuls soon turned into a clearly defined excavation, three feet across and five feet in length.

The ground under the three trees was rocky, and we had to stop often to pull the larger rocks out of the way. At a depth of about three feet, we ran into a large root from one of the trees, and after some coaxing we convinced Rebecca to run home and get an ax to cut the root. If any of the rest of us went home, it might tip someone off, and at the time, little Rebecca was the best candidate for the least notice.

It was almost noon when I found myself standing in a hole, four feet deep in the ground, digging out shovelfuls of black soil, when the shovel struck something hard. It wasn't a rock and it wasn't a root. I started to dig faster, and every shovelful I threw out of the hole confirmed the reality of my wildest dream. I doubt that any experience I had ever had up until then could have compared to the excitement I felt at that moment.

We had struck paydirt. Revealed to me, and to the others gathered anxiously around that small but incredibly important hole we had dug in that forbidden ground, was the top of a chest. It was hard, it was solid, it was very old, and it was *real*.

The old man had been right! *We* had been right. There *was* a treasure—and we had found it! I remember dropping to my knees to scrape away the last of the soil that covered the chest. It was magnificent! It was an old contoured chest with riveted metal bands shaping its top. I couldn't believe it was really happening. I began to dig with my hands, scraping and scooping the dirt from around the chest, looking for the clasp or the lock that held it shut.

And suddenly there it was. I brushed the dirt from the lock so those standing above me could see it. The lock was old and rusted, and it was packed with the soil it had rested in for what must have been a hundred years of hiding. And in its face were three large keyholes.

I shouted for someone to give me something to break it open. I was hurriedly passed a shovel, and I began to attack that old padlock as though it were guarding the greatest treasures of the universe.

It was then that Carmel sounded the alarm. Through my excitement at finding the chest, I still remember her urgent shout telling us that we had been spotted and our father was on his way, headed in our direction. Of any news I could have heard at that moment, that was the worst. To be where we weren't supposed to be was bad enough. To be caught digging holes in the ground was worse. But for anyone under the age of twelve or thirteen, letting an adult find out that we were discovering a treasure would have been unthinkable.

With a menacing adult about to discover our secret, we did the only thing we knew how. We began to cover up the chest. At the time it didn't matter if we had discovered the richest cache of gold and jewels that had ever been found; for the moment, getting rid of the evidence was the only thing that mattered.

By the time our father arrived on the scene, all he saw was a three-by-five-foot hole in the ground, about two or three feet deep. Someone, I forget who, blurted out the first words of an instant and incredible story. We told him that we were digging a pond for goldfish. He didn't buy it, but he couldn't figure out what we were really doing either, so he did the only parentlike thing he could do. He stood there and watched over us as we refilled the entire hole. Then he told us that some suitable punishment would be doled out later, and he made us promise that we would never dig on that property again. We promised that we would not.

I have forgotten what punishment was meted out. I suppose at the time my head was too full of the possibilities of what that chest contained to worry too much about having to do a few extra chores or going to bed that night without eating dinner. I do remember that I was sure my father had gone easier on us because, in addition to telling him that we were digging a pond for fish, I had added that if he didn't punish me, I would go to seminary and become a pastor and help people. He had always hoped that I would. And so the chest, whatever it contained, was once again left to rest, safe from the few inspired young children who had nearly unlocked its secrets, hidden from a world that no longer remembered its existence.

To this day, not one of the original crew of treasure seekers, now all adults, has gone back to find out what was buried in that hole. It wasn't that we were told not to—as adults any of us could have gone back at one time or another to find it again, but we never did. Rebecca grew up and raised a fine family of her own, Carmel went on to write romance novels, and Verne passed away. I never did go to seminary and become the pastor of a quiet little church. I always hoped my father had forgotten the promise about the same time he forgot the incident that inspired it.

All of the treasure hunters have long since moved away from their hometown. For those of us who had almost touched the dream, the story of the treasure is now a story we tell to our children and our grandchildren.

Not long ago I visited that small town where the old wooden chest of unknown contents lies buried in the ground in the center of three tall trees. I flew from my home in another state, rented a car at the airport, found my way from the expressways of the city to the blacktop roads of the open countryside, and headed off into the afternoon sunshine. It was a day much like the summer day many years earlier when my friends and I had had our great adventure. When I arrived in the peaceful little town, I drove along the street I had walked so many times to and from school, and found the place where my childhood home had been. The house I had grown up in wasn't there anymore; a new home had taken its place. The cinder road had become a nicely blacktopped street. The grove of plum trees was gone. It had been replaced by a row of apartments.

No sign of the old haunted house remained. It, too, was gone, and a new three-bedroom home stood in its place. The land around it had been cleared, and the woodsheds and tall dark trees had given way to a well-kept garden surrounded by a fine wooden fence—the kind you buy at a home center and put up on a Saturday afternoon.

But I could not help noticing that in the front part of the neatly trimmed lawn there were three tall trees which had survived. I parked my rented car and got out to say hello to the man who was cutting the grass under those trees. The five large stones were gone, and in their place was a gazebo with white latticework trellises for vines. It looked like the sort of place where the man and his wife could sit and enjoy the evening. I did not tell the man, who was cutting the grass around the gazebo beneath the three tall trees, that about four or five feet under him was an old chest with a rusted three-key lock.

After talking to the man for a few minutes, I thanked him for his time, said good-bye, got in my car, and drove away. A few hours later I was back in a large, crowded city; then I wound my way along the busy freeways, turned in my rental car at the airport, walked through the boarding chute that put me on an airplane destined for a far-off place, and flew away—once again leaving the treasure behind me.

We all have treasures in our lives. Some of us accept them and use them—but most of us leave the best of our selves buried somewhere, waiting to be discovered. *Who knows what could be in that chest?*

For many of us, what we leave behind is the best of us— the best of what we could have been.

I still wish I had broken the lock on that treasure chest way back then. Someday I still may. But what we did then as children is what many of us do throughout our entire adult lives. We get a glimpse of the treasures that are inside our selves. But at the moment when we could break the lock, something makes us cover it back up, leaving behind what *could* have been. Some of us move so far away from where we were, and become so busy with today, that we forget there was ever a treasure in each of our lives in the first place.

I'd like to invite you to go with me on a treasure hunt.

We can find the treasure; that's not the hard part. It will be pointed out to us. We will also learn how to overcome some of the rocks and roots from the past that have kept us from learning the truth. And this time we will learn how to open the lock, open the chest, and begin to live out more of the treasures we find inside our *selves*.

C · H · A · P · T · E · R
TWO

A NEW LOOK
AT OUR "SELVES"

All of us possess treasures within our "selves"—the best of which may still be waiting to be uncovered. A single self can do a surprising number of things in a lifetime. It can be helpful, harmful, practical, absurd, worthwhile, pointless, exceptional, average, marvelous, or mundane. Selves have been known to be courageous at times, and at other times unsure; at one time strong, at another time not. Almost all selves have a nearly unlimited range of expression. Any one of them can be shown to possess an amazing number of possibilities; there is as yet no list that includes every "can do" that a single self *could* do.

Marvelous things, these selves of ours. The day we are born, our selves arrive in relatively good shape, for the most part, uncluttered with notions about what works and what doesn't. These selves come with no biases, no beliefs, no bad habits, no likes or dislikes, no political points of view, no prejudices, no attitudes, no conditioning, no doubts, and no self-limits.

And from the moment our selves arrive, for as long as we have them, they require that we love them and direct them—

11

that we care for them and that we *manage* them. How well our selves do will depend on those two requirements—how *much* we care for them and how *well* we manage them. To live a life that works, to have a healthy self, takes a lot of both.

When our selves first arrive, the responsibility of taking care of them and managing them is given to other people. Then, as the selves learn and grow, the responsibility for caretaking and management is slowly transferred to us. Eventually, for most of us—sometime during the latter part of our teenage years—the preparation of our selves is complete; the gavel is passed on, and, with a sigh of relief, our caretakers relinquish the responsibility of managing us.

In principle, the other people who were in charge of our selves can now relax and step aside, knowing that they have done everything humanly possible to nurture and prepare our selves to operate on their own, with most of the caretaking and all of the management now coming from us. Years later, the selves we were born with are given back to us. *We* are put in charge of our *selves*.

However, there is usually a huge gap between the theory and the practice. If we followed what appeared to be the prearranged order of things, we would, when finally given control over our selves, be able to manage our selves, and thereby our lives, capably and effectively. We would, after all, have been trained as good Self-Managers.

How well do you suppose the average individual's Self-Management skills stack up against what they could be or should be? If you assessed your own Self-Management capabilities, at what level would you be right now? Are you a fully functioning Self-Manager, in control and functioning at your natural optimum? Are you actively managing your self in the right way, using the right methods, and getting the right results? In Chapter Five, with your own Self-Management Survey, you will have a chance to find out how well you're doing.

THE PAST APPROACH

When it comes to Self-Management, most of us haven't been doing very well. We reach maturity grossly under-prepared for what lies ahead. Thereafter we are too busy with the realities of life to go back to the first grade of Self-Management School and start over. If we could go back, would our teachers be any more prepared to help us than they were the first time around?

That problem would certainly leave many of us with a lifelong dilemma: Do we take the selves we were given and get by; do *our* best with selves that were never fully equipped to function at *their* best? Or do we change our selves somehow, after "school" is out, when we are on our own, in the midst of life with its problems and realities?

If we leave the management of our selves to chance, as we did in the past, we can be certain that we will fare no better in the future. Unless we do something for our selves now, even if it might seem too late to begin changing things, we are destined to live out our lives unmanaged and unfulfilled.

That makes Self-Management pretty powerful—perhaps the most powerful influence in the success of *anything* we undertake. If that is true, it would make sense to learn a little more about it. Exactly what is Self-Management? Does it work—and *how* does it work? Where was Self-Management when you got your early training in how to cope with life? Why isn't it being taught more in schools and homes? Can anyone learn Self-Management? Are *you* ready?

By the end of this book, you will not only have the answers to those questions, but you will be consciously and *un*consciously using Self-Management tools that could create more *life* in your life, more *self* in your self. You may find that you surprise yourself—or perhaps your *self,* with the right coaching, will start surprising you.

Perhaps you share the sentiment of a friend of mine who had made the decision to get himself and his life firmly under control. He told me, "This is the life I have to live; I might as well get it right." If that is what you would like to do, then let us begin. I think you'll enjoy the journey.

C · H · A · P · T · E · R

THREE

WHY WE DO WHAT WE DO

One of the most important discoveries in recent years has been our understanding of the role that our own casual *thinking* plays in the shaping of our lives.

Throughout thousands of years we believed that thoughts, for the most part, meant nothing at all. We believed that thoughts were harmless, bodiless, energyless bits of consciousness that had no substance and no life of their own. And for all that time, we were wrong.

Our thoughts, each and every one of them, are much more than we believed them to be—so much more, in fact, that it is only now, as we enter the age of computer intelligence, that we are beginning to discover just how important each *human thought* actually is.

Far from thoughts being vague "nothings" that go nowhere and do nothing, neuroscientists have learned that thoughts are electrical impulses that trigger electrical and chemical switches in the brain. Thoughts are not just psychological in nature, they are *physiological*—electrochemical triggers that direct and affect the chemical activity in the brain.

When given an electrical command—a thought—the brain immediately does several things: It responds to the thought by releasing appropriate control chemicals into the body, and it alerts the central nervous system to any required response or action.

At the same time, as a response to the same thought, the brain searches its memory files, finds the proper place to record any necessary information gleaned from the thought, creates a mental or an internal physiological reaction based on earlier information already stored there, and stores any new information that might be of future value.

While we are thinking the thought, we are not consciously aware of what the brain is doing with it. Where the brain puts the new information and what it makes of it will be determined by what it gleans from our genetic programming, our *previous input* and by *how we direct the new thought at the time we think it*.

SENDING SIGNALS

To simplify the process we can look at a thought as a short burst of electrical current that sends a signal to the brain. The central control board in the brain picks up the signal as a directive, and it responds by alerting the necessary chemical centers in the brain to take the necessary action—to put things in motion chemically, electrically, and physically to deal with whatever the thought triggered and thereby told the brain to do.

The thought also contains impressions that the brain may want to store; so it instantly analyzes those impressions and imprints them in one or more of several storage areas. Later, long after the chemical response to the thought is gone, the brain continues to hold the impressions it received for future use. In some cases the impressions are stored as feelings, as an example; in other cases the impressions are stored as visual pictures.

In every case the brain simply records what it receives. It makes no difference if the information was true, false, good, bad, important, or unimportant. Since the brain is an organ, just as the heart is an organ, it performs a specific activity in a certain way. The brain just does what it was designed to do. If it is working properly, it will function in precisely the same way year after year, second after second, for an entire lifetime, receiving, processing, storing, and acting upon information.

IT ISN'T MAGIC

The brain, and that facet of the brain we call the *mind,* are not magic. The brain may be complex but, whether we accept it or not, it is an organ that does what it was intended to do. If we treat it right, the brain will do astounding things for us. It will keep us alive and healthy, help us stay out of trouble, work tirelessly to help us reach our goals, and help us live a life of value and attainment. It will store a vast amount of useful information that will keep us on track and in tune with life around us. But if we treat it *wrong,* it will do none of those things right; it will work against us instead of for us.

It makes no difference to the brain whether we understand it or not, whether we believe it or not. The essential function and activity of the human brain are no longer topics of speculation and debate. We know that the brain is an incredibly well-engineered instrument created to function in a specific way. That is what it does; it has no choice.

That's important for us to know, because how the brain operates has a lot to do with how the *self* operates. It is through the brain that we care for, command, and communicate with our selves. If we try to manage the self in a way that is out of step with how the brain functions—chemically and electrically—the self isn't going to get the message. And we won't get the right results.

The analogy of the human brain as a personal computer is an accurate one. The brain receives, processes, stores, and acts on the input received from the senses in much the same way that a computer receives its programming, processes it, stores it, and acts on it. The subconscious mind is programmed much like a computer is programmed, and like the computer, the subconscious mind will do only what it is programmed to do.

THE LONG-PLAYING RECORD

Imagine that the subconscious mind acts like a phonograph record. The day we were born each of us started life with a shiny, clean record, one on which no grooves had ever been recorded.

Then from the first day, as we grew, each word we heard, and each thought we thought, recorded a groove in that record. Some thoughts, those that were fed to us again and again, were recorded over and over, cutting grooves that would prove to be deep and permanent. In time, even our own self-directions—images and thoughts we had about ourselves—became part of the indelible recording that would become a permanent part of the program we gave to our subconscious minds.

As we grew, it made no difference to our subconscious minds whether what we were saying or accepting about our selves was true or false. Our subconscious minds, just like desk-top computers, simply accepted what we and others programmed into them—whether the information was accurate or inaccurate, healthy or unhealthy, helpful or unhelpful.

It is precisely because of how our brains work that we become creatures of habit. Because of our programming we form patterns—repetitive styles, actions, and thoughts—in our subconscious minds. And we tend to repeat those behavior patterns that are the most strongly programmed. If you have read my book *What to Say When You Talk to Your Self,* you will be familiar with just how that programming works and how effective it is. Because 75 percent or more of our early programming was of the negative kind, we automatically followed suit with our own self-talk—our own self-programming of the same negative kind.

We do receive good programs, of course, but not enough of them. The result is that we grow to maturity with some of the most inappropriate and self-hindering programs imaginable stuck permanently in our subconscious minds, where they will affect every action we will ever take and every thought we will ever think, for the rest of our lives.

The way we live our lives is the result of the sum total of those programs—those thoughts and self-directives that were so unknowingly handed to us by everyone in general and by our selves in particular.

The end result has been that each of us is living with an endless battery of internal programs, that the brain, at this very moment, is working to act out. That is what it was programmed to do. *It has no choice.* Acting on your instructions is what your brain was designed to do. As long as it is functioning properly, that is exactly what it will continue to do. *It makes no difference to your brain whether you have given it good programs or bad.* The full awesome power of your brain will see to it that you live out the programs that are currently resting in your subconscious mind.

A MOST IMPORTANT CHOICE

What we program into our subconscious minds has always been up to us, even from a very young age; we just didn't know it at the time. Once we become aware of the process by which the indifferent, methodical functioning of the brain actually works, what gets programmed *next* is more up to each of us than ever before.

Your subconscious mind will not care where that programming comes from or how it gets it. It will just continue to accept the input that is fed to it—right or wrong, for better or worse. The programming that you accept from others, and the conscious and unconscious directives, pictures, feelings, and thoughts that you transmit to your self, will find a place in your own internal control center.

Together, *those directions, thoughts, and images will continue to create in advance, or influence on the spot, every response, attitude, and action that will be a part of you and your future.*

In fact, *right now,* your personal programs are creating everything about you short of your genetic structure and whatever traits may have been handed down to you by your ancestors. When you were born, what you arrived here with was up to someone else to manage and take care of. What you did with it in the past was up to what was tucked away in the subconscious programs that were in control. What you do with your self from here on out will be influenced by what you decide to do next and what you actually do about it—it will be up to every new self-direction you give your self.

That gives each of us an exciting but incredibly important choice. That's why those who say, "My future is up to me!" are not being vain or humanistic. Instead they are joyously recognizing the fact that they now have the option of seeing that their future moves in the direction of their own choosing.

Those who learn to be in control of their own *selves*, by consciously controlling their own self-directives, are the only ones who have any real control at all over their earthly destinies.

The alternative is to stand aside and let the world do what it will with the one thing in this life that was left entirely in your safekeeping—your *self*. If you do not take personal responsibility for the care and feeding of your own subconscious mind, if you do not manage your own self, it will be managed by the whims of the world around you. *The brain does not care which path you choose*. It will work just as hard to please any master it is given.

WHAT WE DO KNOW CAN HELP

What we don't know can do more than hurt us. What we did not understand about our own minds in the past was exactly what caused us to have so many of our problems— problems which we have literally created for our selves.

Fortunately, neuroscientists, medical researchers, and psychologists did not leave us stranded with the impossible problem of recognizing what went wrong without figuring out what to do about it. Research and insight have not only shown us the problem—they have given us the solution. The same mental processes which once held us back can now be used to move us ahead.

FOUR

OUR SELF-TALK OF THE PAST

In order to find out what sorts of programs will work best for you—and which of your old programs you might want to change or replace—you need only look at the old self-talk that you have been giving your self in the past. Whatever that self-talk was, you can be sure that you are living out the results of it every day.

Since birth, each of us has collected an overwhelming number of self-talk programs. Some of those programs have been good. Some of them have done us no good at all.

Ellen Brooks attended a seminar I was conducting on Self-Talk.* She was a middle-aged woman who had just become a grandparent for the first time. I asked the members of the audience to share some examples of their old self-talk

---

*To differentiate between previous improper or misdirected forms of self-talk, and the newer forms of constructive Self-Talk, the old form of self-talk will appear in *lower*case throughout this book. The new form of Self-Talk will appear in *upper*case.

with the rest of the group, and Ellen was one of the first to raise her hand. "Ever since I was a little girl," she said, "my mother told me that when I got older and became a grandmother I would be overweight—just like my grandmother was."

The prediction Ellen's mother made had proved to be true. Within months of becoming a grandparent, Ellen had gained weight and was having trouble getting back to the healthier weight which she had maintained for years previously. "It wasn't just my age or my life-style that did it for me," Ellen said. "I gained the weight because I believed I would, and I told my self for years that that's what I would do."

A radio listener, Doug Spencer, called in to a radio talk show that I was appearing on in the Midwest. "I've always told my self that I can't handle money," he told me. "Every time the subject of money came up I told my self I was no good with finances. I actually convinced my self. It turned out to be true."

On another radio show a woman called in to say that the discussion we were having on "programming" children had started her thinking about some of the things she had said to her own four children when they were young. The youngest had not done as well in school as his older brother and sisters had. "I used to tell my youngest son that he just wasn't cut out for school so he would always have to try harder," the caller said. "I even told him that he would never be able to go to college because he just wasn't college material. Eventually he became convinced that I was right. I've learned that he was just as capable as the others, but he was the only one of the four who never attended college."

I received a letter from a secretary in which she said that she had continually told her self she was not attractive, that her personality was not as good or as bright as the other people in her office, and that she was not well liked. "I'm always telling my self that I'm not good enough, or that I just can't do as well as someone else," she wrote. "If there is a chance of moving up in the company or getting a raise in pay, I'm the first one to tell me that I won't make it."

Of the hundreds of letters I receive, I am always amazed at the number of good, everyday people who have burdened

themselves with that same kind of negative self-direction—
the wrong kind of self-talk. One writer spoke for a lot of
others when he wrote, "I can't tell you how many negative
things (mostly untrue) I grew up learning to say to my self.
I've told my self I can't exercise, that I put things off, that I
never get anyplace on time, and that I can't even talk to my
wife without starting an argument."

I even receive letters from schoolchildren who tell similar stories about their own self-talk. A junior-high-school
student wrote, "I never thought I could do anything right. I
kept telling my self that the only thing I would ever do was
get into trouble."

Another letter, from an elderly member of the clergy
who had spent most of his years as a teacher, was so moving
that I phoned him to talk to him. As I had learned from
reading his letter, the old gentleman was saddened and trou-
bled by his "lost years" of poor programs. "Why didn't they
tell us how to talk to our selves years ago, when I was young,
when I could have made a difference? For sixty years I could
have been teaching my self and others to talk to our selves
differently," he said. "But until now I never knew what our
own self-talk does to us. Look at all the problems I created
for my self. Think of what I *could* have done!"

At the time these people were saying the wrong things to
themselves, none of them had any idea that they were literally programming themselves to believe those things.

In reading the many letters I receive and when talking to
people throughout my travels, I have often been reminded of
some of the self-talk *I* had used in my own past. I sometimes
wonder how many of the problems I have encountered in the
past were problems which I literally *created* for my self. Each
time I ask an audience to share examples of their own past
self-talk, I hear some of the same *wrong* self-directions that I
have used myself.

Few of us escape the habit of negative self-talk. And the
self-talk we learn from others—and soon begin to use ourselves—can be as simple as an unspoken doubt or fear, or as
major as a well-rehearsed script of clear untrue self-state-
ments to ourselves about what we *cannot* do, what we cannot
achieve, what won't work, and why we cannot live more of
the better life that we would like to live.

AN ENDLESS LIST OF UNNECESSARY SELF-TALK

There are countless, almost unnoticed, but powerfully important self-talk thoughts and phrases that many of us, *unknowingly*, have used to program our selves.

How can we possibly expect the best from our selves when we tell our "selves" things like *"I'm going nowhere at work"; "It's just not my day"; "I just can't do this"; "Every time I try to talk to him (or her) we have an argument"; "I have a problem with my weight"; "I just know she (or he) won't like me"; "Why should I try, it probably won't work out anyway"; "I just can't seem to get caught up"; "I have the worst memory"; "I'm no good at . . ."; "I never seem to get a break"; "Just this once won't hurt"; "I find something on sale and I can't help myself"; "I don't know what's wrong with me today"; "I've tried, but I just can't!"*

Those are examples of some of the statements that program us. They are the kinds of programs which guide and direct us throughout our lives. They describe us to our selves in ways that work against us, and we will act them out in ways that harm us or hold us back.

How much better programming we would give our selves if, instead of saying things in ways that set our words against us, we turned each phrase around and let it work *for* us. In the above examples, each of the "old" self-talk phrases would then become "new" Self-Talk that sounds like this:

"I'm making progress at work"; "Today is a great day for me!"; "I can handle this"; "Every time I talk to him (or her) we communicate better"; "I'm getting in control of my weight"; "I just know she (or he) is going to like me"; "I am willing to try, there's a good chance it will work"; "I'm getting caught up on everything"; "I have an excellent memory"; "I'm good at . . ."; "I'm fortunate things go my way"; "Just this once I won't"; "Even if I find something on sale, I'm never tempted to spend what I shouldn't"; "I feel especially good about my self today"; and "I'll keep trying and I'll get it yet!"

The decision to program our selves with words which cause problems or failures in life, or with words which give us confidence and self-belief, is up to each of us. *That is our Self-Talk. That is how we manage our selves.*

I am often inspired by the number of letters I receive from hospitals, colleges, state health boards, prisons, drug-treatment centers, medical research groups, and other organizations that are studying and teaching the uses of Self-Talk. An example of these is a medical research group in California which is scientifically validating the effects of Self-Talk and attitudes on the human immune system. This organization, like other research groups throughout the United States, clearly sees a strong relationship between Self-Talk and health—with Self-Talk being a contributing factor in the development of the immunological—disease fighting—capability of the human body.

Throughout history we've been told that we can assist our selves to be well simply by what we think and what we say when we talk to our selves. But it has taken modern medical science to prove that the advice we were given was grounded in scientific fact. I remember a high-school classmate of mine was constantly being told by her mother, "Sandy, you don't look well today. Are you sure you feel all right?" It's no wonder Sandy stayed home sick more often than the rest of us. She was programmed to be not well!

Just imagine what you have told yourself about your "self." What have you learned to believe about *you* that may not have been true at all? What words of programming have you unknowingly accepted from others and, just as unknowingly, accepted from your self? Have you been telling your self the winning words of self-belief, or have you been repeating words of uncertainty or disbelief? Do you criticize yourself or do you tell your "self" that you are capable of doing better—and that you are well on your way to doing it?

We will never know how many times a man or a woman failed or felt defeated because that person never learned to change the words of his or her self-talk. We will never know what wars could have been avoided, what children could have grown up differently, what lives of frustration could have been, instead, lives of achievement and joy.

There is no way to calculate what the simple change of self-directions from "I can't" to "I can" could have meant in the lives of the untold millions of hopeful individuals who have gone before us.

Self-Talk is self-control, self-direction, and self-responsibility—in their simplest, most natural form. How many people do you know who would be happier, more productive, and more self-confident, and feel better about themselves if they learned the skills of self-direction and Self-Management? It is our own Self-Talk that can do that for us.

Throughout the world, how many tens of thousands of self-defeating words are uttered to tens of thousands of receptive, unknowing minds each day? The answer is, of course, *millions*—perhaps billions. Few have learned to program themselves with the best of themselves. Many have learned to program themselves with the worst. And most have never learned to think about their self-talk at all.

I have often thought that all of us would have been a little bit better off if we had learned, almost from birth, a few simple extra "truths" about our selves. Those truths wouldn't get in the way of religion, or family, or upbringing of any kind. They would *add* to our learning in a most important way. And they would give each of us something extra to help us along the way.

Those truths would be worded something like this:

> *I like who I am, and I'm glad to be me.*

> *I'm glad to be alive, and I've decided to be the best "me" that I can be.*

> *Today is a good day. Today is the day that I choose to be my best and to do my best. I'll have other good days, too, but today is special—and so am I!*

> *I've made the decision to win in my life. I'm in control, on top, in tune, in touch, and nothing can stand between me and the goals I've set for my self.*

> *I can do it. Just watch me and I'll prove it!*

Those are not the lofty words of some visionary or dreamer. Quite the opposite. They are examples of the simple, practical self-directions that help us see our selves, and life around us, in a more effective way each day.

After having studied Self-Talk and self-programming for many years, I suspect that those few words, repeated often enough, indelibly etched in the recorded files of the mind, would have an effect on almost anyone. But as we shall see, Self-Talk goes far beyond the repetition of a few simple words of self-programming.

For most of us, our past self-talk has not always worked well for us. If it had, we wouldn't be looking for something else. Few of us escaped early programming by others. And most of us were not offered an alternative. The Self-Talk Solution is a step in the right direction. It shows you how to look at the self-talk you used in the past, and it offers you a way to make worthwhile changes in your Self-Talk in the future.

FIVE

TAKING INVENTORY OF YOUR SELF

There is a story of an old man and a young boy who lived in ancient times. The old man was named Sartebus, and the boy was named Kim. Kim was an orphan, living on his own, making his way from village to village in search of food and a roof over his head. But most important of all, even more than his search for a full stomach and a comfortable dry place to sleep, Kim was looking for something else—he was searching for a *reason*. "Why," he wondered, "do we travel throughout our lives in search of something we cannot find? Why must things be as difficult as they are? Do we make them so ourselves, or is it just meant to be that we should struggle as we do?"

These were wise thoughts for a boy as young as Kim, but it was just that kind of thinking that caused him to find along the way an old man, traveling the same road, who, Kim thought, might help him with an answer or two.

The old man was carrying on his back a large, covered, woven basket that appeared to be very heavy, especially for someone as old and weary as he was. When they stopped to rest beside a small brook along the road, the old man wearily settled his basket on the ground. To Kim it looked as though the man carried all of his worldly goods in that one basket; it seemed to be much heavier than even a much younger, stronger man could carry very far.

"What is in your basket that makes it so heavy?" Kim asked Sartebus. "I would be happy to carry it for you. After all, I am young and strong, and you are tired." "It is nothing you could carry for me," answered the old man. "This is something I must carry for myself." And he added, "One day, you will walk your own road and carry a basket as weighted as mine."

Over many days and many roads, Kim and the old man walked many miles together. And although Kim often asked old Sartebus questions about why men must toil as they do, Kim did not learn from him any of the answers, nor could he learn, try as he might, what treasure of such great weight was in the basket the old man carried.

Sometimes late at night, at the end of a long day's journey, Kim would lie quietly, pretending to sleep, listening to the old man sorting through the contents of his basket by the flickering light from a small fire, and talking quietly to himself. But in the morning, as always, he would say nothing.

It was only when Sartebus could walk no more, and he lay down to rest for the last time, that he told young Kim his secret. In their last few hours together, he gave to Kim not only the answer to the riddle of the basket he carried, but the answer to why men toil as they do.

"In this basket," Sartebus said, "are all of the things I believed about my self which were not true. They are the stones that weighted down my journey. On my back I have carried the weight of every pebble of doubt, every grain of the sand of uncertainty, and every millstone of misdirection I have collected along my way. Without these I could have gone so far. I could have lived a life of the dreams I saw in my mind. But with them I have ended up here, at the end of my journey." And without even unwrapping the braided cords that bound the basket to him, the old man closed his eyes and quietly went to sleep for the last time.

Before Kim himself went to sleep that night, he untied each cord that bound the basket to the old man and, lifting it free, carefully set it on the ground. When he had done this, he just as carefully untied the leather straps that held the woven cover in place, and lifted it aside. Perhaps because he had been looking for an answer to his own question, he was not at all surprised at what he found inside. The basket, which had weighted old Sartebus down for so long, was empty.

WHAT DO YOU CARRY WITH YOU?

All of us have collected thoughts and beliefs and ideas about our selves that weigh us down and hold us back from reaching so many of the opportunities that life holds in store for us.

How do we find out what is in our basket? What is the weight that is holding *us* down? What limitations about our selves have we *imagined* to be true when they may not be true at all?

Sartebus, unfortunately, did not know that he could throw away his imagined millstones. He was left, instead, to sit at night, inventorying his limitations and wishing things could be better.

YOUR INVENTORY OF IMAGINED LIMITATIONS

In order to learn some of what your subconscious believes about you now, it will help to ask your self some questions and give your self some honest answers. If you would like to know what kinds of things you are saying to your self *unconsciously,* you will find the answer in what you say to your self *consciously.*

What you hear yourself say to your "self" out loud is only the tip of the iceberg; what goes on underneath is mammoth compared with what we can see on the surface. For every conscious, *noticed* thought you have, there are many more thoughts that are never noticed at all. Those unseen or unheard thoughts are like a chorus of a thousand voices, all echoing the same kinds of thoughts in the recesses of your subconscious mind.

Your *conscious* thoughts (and words) are reflections of the *un*conscious programs that create them. If your conscious self-directions are productive, healthy, and work for

you, your other *un*conscious self-directions will also be the
kind which are healthy and work for you. If you find self-
directions in your conscious thoughts that create doubts, or
picture you as being less than what you *could* be, then you
can be sure that those same misdirections are being mirrored
many thousands of times over by the unconscious thoughts
of your subconscious mind.

You can examine your own self-directions and find out
what they are. By asking your self even a few questions you
can get an accurate picture of how you really see your self in
your subconscious mind.

What kinds of self-directions are unconsciously in control of your life right now? In the following self-survey, if you
complete each of the statements accurately and honestly, you
will get an idea of what you carry in your own storehouse of
self-thoughts. This survey is not intended to tell you everything you carry with you. But it will help you take an honest
look at your own inventory of limitations—so that you can
have a chance at doing something about them.

If you do not wish to write in the pages of this book,
make a photocopy of the survey pages so that you can write
in the blanks. If you cannot or do not wish to write out your
choices, read the statements aloud and fill in the blanks out
loud also. The survey statements are designed to give you a
better understanding of some of your own important styles of
Self-Management. Take your time. Be honest. And complete
every one of the statements.

The Self-Management Survey

Part 1—Your General Self-Management Style
*Complete each of the statements below with
one of the following:* **Always, Usually, Occasionally,
Seldom,** *or* **Never.**

1. I _____ feel that I am in control of
most of the important areas of my life.
2. I am _____ a "positive" person.
3. I _____ get depressed about
things.

4. I _____ feel that much of what happens in my life is up to chance.

5. I believe that my life is _____ determined entirely by outside circumstances and that I _____ have control over what happens to me.

6. I _____ feel that most of what happens in my life is up to me.

7. I am _____ aware of my own self-talk and I am _____ conscious of my own self-direction.

8. I am _____ upset or frustrated by things that I cannot change or do anything about.

9. I _____ have a strong self-image. I _____ like who I am today.

10. I _____ wake up in good spirits and eager to deal with the day ahead.

11. I _____ get upset when I am delayed in traffic.

12. Other people would _____ describe me as successful.

13. I am _____ good at dealing with and solving problems.

14. I _____ set goals and follow through with them.

15. I am _____ organized and I _____ get things done on time.

16. I _____ have a sense of who I am and where I am going in life.

17. I _____ feel that I am special, unique, and in control of my self and my life.

18. I _____ take personal and full responsibility for my self, my actions, and my future.

19. I _____ control my own thoughts and I _____ allow myself to worry.

20. I consider that I am _____ a good Self-Manager.

There are hundreds of questions you could answer about how you manage your self. But the above questions give you a picture of how well, at least until now, you have been doing in the area of *general* Self-Management.

When you complete the survey statements, look for a trend in your responses. If, for instance, you typically complete the statements such as "I _____ have a sense of who I am and where I am going in life" with an immediate and unquestioned *"Always,"* your confidence level land your Self-Management skills are likely to be high.

If, on the other hand, you find that you completed statements like "I am _____ aware of my own self-talk and I am _____ conscious of my own self-direction," with any hesitancy or with *"Occasionally,"* *"Seldom,"* or *"Never,"* you are not exercising as much Self-Management as you could or should be.

Let's take a look at another area of Self-Management. The statements in Part 1 of the survey were general; they dealt with your attitudes about how much control you feel you exercise over broad areas and circumstances of your life. Now, let's be more specific. In the following survey section, each statement asks that you review your Self-Management in your work life, or your life outside the home.

Self-Management Survey

Part 2—Work Life and Career
Respond to these statements below just as you did in Part I—accurately and honestly. Either directly in the book, on a photocopy of the survey, or in your mind, complete each statement with one of the following: **Always, Usually, Occasionally, Seldom,** *or* **Never.**

1. I am _____ an achiever. I _____ do the best that I am capable of doing.
2. I am _____ determined to achieve my aims.
3. Defeat _____ sets me back or stops me from getting the job and my objectives accomplished.

4. I _____ feel that I have the skill and the confidence to excel in my work.

5. I _____ have a winning attitude about my self and my role in life.

6. I _____ feel that I have good ideas and that others are _____ interested in what I have to say.

7. I feel that I _____ express my self well.

8. I _____ waste time and I _____ plan my time to get the most accomplished in the time I have.

9. I _____ do my best at any task or job that I accept.

10. I _____ do everything I need to do when I need to do it.

11. I _____ feel that I have self-worth and value, whether in my work or anything that I do.

12. I feel that I am _____ forced to live my life by the dictates, the demands, or the expectations of others.

13. I _____ look forward at the opportunities in front of me and I _____ look back at what I may have left behind.

14. I am _____ alert, sharp, aware, in tune, and on top of things.

15. I _____ feel that I am an intelligent, capable person and that I can accomplish anything I put my mind to.

16. I _____ feel that people like me and like to be around me.

17. I _____ spend time improving my skills or preparing my self for new opportunities.

18. I _____ feel the self-assurance that nothing can stand in the way of my goals or my success.

19. I _____ see risks as a necessary part of my achievement and I am _____ certain of my ability to meet them and surpass them.

20. I feel that I am _____ personally in control of what happens in my work and how well I will do.

YOUR RESPONSES ARE THE BEST INDICATION OF THE KIND OF SELF-MANAGEMENT THAT IS GUIDING YOU NOW

Your responses to the above statements indicate the Self-Management programs that are currently operating in a variety of ways in your life. If your responses tell you that you are happy and in tune with your job, career, or daily work or routine, then listen to what you are saying to your self—the Self-Talk that is directing you in the right direction—and do more of it. If you are not as satisfied as you would like to be, your responses will give you some good examples of the kind of self-talk that could be holding you back.

If, for example, you were to complete statement 18 to read: "I *never* feel the self-assurance that nothing can stand in the way of my goals or my success," this is a perfect example of self-talk that stops you from reaching your goal.

If you were to complete statement 12 to read: "I feel that I am *usually* forced to live my life by the dictates, the demands, or the expectations of others," this is exactly the sort of self-talk that creates a problem.

The accurate responses that you give when you complete the survey statements directly characterize or duplicate the kind of self-talk you have been using.

If you want to know what your *un*conscious self-talk has been, write the survey statements, with your responses, on a piece of paper: If your responses show a negative pattern, the list will indicate precisely the self-talk *that contributed to the problem in the first place*.

By recognizing the *old* self-talk that controls you now, you learn which *new* Self-Talk will counteract the old. The statements you've completed show the self-talk you've been using—and that, in turn, tells you what new kind of Self-Talk you should replace it with.

Let's look at another section of your personal self-talk

inventory that makes a few statements about your family, home, and personal life.

Self-Management Survey

Part 3—Family, Home, and Personal Life
Complete each statement with one of the following: **Always, Usually, Occasionally, Seldom,** *or* **Never.**

1. My personal relationships are _____ warm, meaningful, and rewarding.

2. I am _____ able to express my feelings toward others and I am _____ patient and understanding of their expressions toward me.

3. I _____ make friends easily and I have great respect for the friendships I make.

4. People can _____ rely on me in any relationship.

5. I am _____ honest, sincere, and open in my thoughts and opinions.

6. I _____ feel good about my self and I _____ experience fulfillment in all areas of my life.

7. I am _____ in touch with my own feelings and I am _____ considerate of the feelings of others.

8. I _____ have a high level of energy.

9. I _____ have plenty of ambition and I _____ meet every opportunity with drive and ambition.

10. I _____ keep my self in excellent physical condition.

11. I _____ program my mind with positive instructions to keep me fit, energetic, and filled with youthful enthusiasm.

12. Good health _____ comes naturally to me.

13. I _____ eat and drink only those foods that are beneficial to my physical health and mental well-being.

14. I am _____ calm and confident. I _____ have the self-assurance of winning in my life.

15. I _____ control the stress in my life.

16. I am _____ a good listener.

17. I feel that I am _____ successful in creating the future that I really want.

18. I _____ feel that I am living up to my best expectations of my self.

19. I feel that my personal life is _____ under control.

20. I am _____ happy with the direction of my life and I feel that I _____ spend my time in the very best possible way.

WHAT YOU CARRY WITH YOU IS UP TO YOU

As you will learn, not only is it your choice to carry or *not* to carry a heavy load of limitations around with you—but it is also your choice to do something about them. Get rid of them! Throw them out! Do more than sit with your thoughts before bedtime like old Sartebus did, keeping an inventory of what you cannot do.

If you would like to make a change, you can. There is a natural path you can follow. It is a path that leads you from the unconscious programs of the past—to more successful Self-Management in the future.

SIX

NEW TECHNOLOGY AND THE SUBCONSCIOUS MIND

In the past few years, researchers have uncovered some surprising new information about the brain, and about the inner workings of that facet of the brain called the *mind*. We have also learned much about the synergistic process within the brain known as the *subconscious* mind.

One of the important characteristics which researchers have learned about the subconscious is that it follows specific *"rules."* The human brain is a physiological organ—a physical, biological mechanism that follows physical laws. The subconscious mind, which is a facet of the physical brain, follows those same rules.

We learn a great deal about why we do what we do, when we understand the rules of the subconscious mind. The subconscious may be the control center that guides and directs us, but it does so with rules of its own to follow—rules which are physiological in nature, and universal.

These are the rules which tell you why your conditioning and programming work as they do, and, as a result, why you do many of the things that you do. They are a few of the most widely accepted characteristics, or tenets, of the subconscious mind and they form the basis for most of the currently accepted theories regarding Self-Management:

10 RULES THAT MANAGE SELF-MANAGEMENT

1. The human brain is a physiological organ which, through a specific electrochemical process, collects, processes, stores, and acts on information it receives.

2. Information presented to the subconscious mind triggers both a physiological response and a psychological response.

3. Any information presented to the subconscious mind is always linked to, and affected by, previously stored information.

4. The subconscious mind is a neutral mechanism which responds to information without subjective regard for its accuracy or its value.

5. The subconscious mind holds no beliefs or biases other than those which it receives as a result of its programming.

6. When faced with two or more programs that are in conflict with each other, the subconscious will attempt to act on the program which is the strongest.

7. The strength of the program is influenced by the number of times the same or similar information is presented.

8. The strength of the program is influenced by the perceived importance of the program source.

9. The strength of the program is influenced by the amount of emotion associated with the program.

10. The subconscious mind will, at all times, attempt to act on its dominant operative program.

To help you explore how to better manage your self, let's take a closer look at each of these "rules" of the subconscious that are behind your own Self-Management.

1. The Human Brain Is a Physiological Organ Which, Through a Specific Electrochemical Process, Collects, Processes, Stores, and Acts on Information It Receives.

The key to this tenet is that the brain is an organ that is set up to perform very *specific* functions in a very *specific* manner. There are times when motivational trainers and self-improvement writers imply that the brain possesses some kind of mystical magic and can do anything.

I agree that the brain is a miraculous organ that does its job in marvelous and wonderful ways; it is without a doubt the most incredible of all earthly scientific wonders. But it still plays by the rules. Along with keeping your life-support systems running, your brain tirelessly collects information and acts on it in a predictable way, minute by minute, year by year, each moment of your life.

That fact is the key to the process of Self-Management. It is very reassuring to know that if you learn the rules, give your brain the right directions, and keep it healthy, it will do its job in the right way.

2. Information Presented to the Subconscious Mind Triggers Both a Physical Response and a Psychological Response.

This means that you are an individual composed of both "body" and "mind." You are made up of physical (chemical) parts, as well as mental (psychological) parts. Any input the brain receives affects you both physically *and* mentally. Every thought you think has an effect on the *entire* "you" whether you are aware of it or not—and, most of the time, you are not.

While your brain is responding to the input, or thought, in a *physical* way, your mind is also processing the thought as part of a new or existing program.

When a young boy, for example, is hit by a softball while

sliding into home plate, his *brain* is operating automatically, at high speed, to move the child out of the way, protect him, check for injuries, and send a fresh batch of oxygen to the point of contact with the ball.

In the same instant that the boy's brain is unconsciously responding by recognizing that he got hit, his mind searches through its memory programs for every scrap of information it has previously stored on being hit by a round, relatively hard object moving at high speed.

Assuming that our young ballplayer was not hurt, and depending on what programs his subconscious dredges up, the child may jump to his feet in triumph, he may start yelling at whomever he thinks threw the ball, or he may wince in pain and start shedding a few tears if his subconscious tells him that would be the most rewarding action to take.

What the boy does, beginning the split second the ball strikes him, will be to react *physically* and *psychologically*, with every part of his brain and mind working together to achieve their intended result.

In another example, let's imagine that it's early in the morning on the day when you're leaving on vacation, and your alarm clock has just gone off.

From the moment your brain perceives the sound of the alarm clock, your subconscious mind will be rapidly sorting every program it contains about such diverse subjects as *this* vacation, *past* vacations, getting out of bed, things to do, things you didn't get done but should have, what the weather is like outside, how you feel physically, and how you feel about getting up at this unreasonable hour of the morning.

Every preprogrammed notion you have about each of these things will affect you, even in those first brief moments. The effects will be both *physiological* and *psychological*. The events of the moment, along with the chemical makeup of your mind, tied to your programs of the past, will determine whether you enthusiastically leap out of bed in anticipation or shrink back under the covers.

Your physical body will receive specific instructions from your brain, triggering the release of precisely measured chemicals, each one with specific tasks to accomplish. Inside the brain itself, message conduits will be alive with tens of thousands of electrical impulses, routing information to and from different control centers in the brain, switching millions of cells into light-speed activity.

If all works well, if the previous programs permit, and if your brain is in reasonably good working order on that particular day, the end result of your abrupt awakening will be that you get up, meet the day, and get moving.

The *physical* organ of the brain did not accomplish this all by itself. Nor did the programs of the *subconscious* mind get you going all by themselves.

Every input, every thought you think, affects the combined facets of brain and mind. These integral facets working *together* cause you to take the action and achieve the result.

3. Any Information Presented to the Subconscious Mind Is Always Linked to, and Affected by, Previously Stored Information.

Every thought you think is passed by all the previous programs you have stored—in a *comparison, analysis,* and *placement* process that takes place in your subconscious mind the moment the input is received. When the telephone rings at midnight, the thought "Who could that be?" is accompanied by an immediate, massive search of your subconscious program banks. Even the tone of your voice when you answer the phone may betray fear, hope, excitement, or dread, depending on how you have already been programmed to react to a call at that time of night.

When you meet someone for the first time, at the same moment you are saying, "Hello, it's nice to meet you," you are unconsciously collecting, sifting, and comparing thousands of mental notes that may directly or indirectly relate to that person. Every one of those mental notes is based on beliefs, attitudes, and feelings that were *previously* collected and stored by your subconscious mind.

The result, of course, is that what you think about this new acquaintance on first meeting has more to do with *previous* programs than with actual, but yet unknown, information about the individual you are just now meeting.

This doesn't mean that you should not trust your first impressions. It means that your first impressions are for the most part actually *old impressions* applied to new situations.

In your subconscious mind, no single thought or piece of information stands on its own.

Any new program you receive is always compared with, and modified by, every old program you have stored.

4. The Subconscious Mind Is a Neutral Mechanism Which Responds to Information Without Subjective Regard for Its Accuracy or Its Value.

By itself, the subconscious mind just doesn't *care* what you tell it. It isn't the least bit interested in figuring out what is right and what is wrong. It will, if you program it properly, alert you to things that you *tell* it are right or wrong. But on its own, your subconscious mind does not make value judgments; it takes the information you give it and acts on it.

The subconscious mind does not differentiate between *factual* reality and *imagined* reality. That is why you can think you are sick when you are not—or end up *thinking* yourself into actually becoming ill. That is why you can believe you are unlucky, not smart enough, incapable, destined to be overweight, poor, or below average, when none of those programs is actually true about you—until you begin to believe them yourself.

But it also explains why you can *exchange* "bad" programming for "good." Since your subconscious mind is designed to accept information *as it is given,* you can present it with new programs which will override or replace the past programs that have worked against you.

5. The Subconscious Mind Holds No Beliefs or Biases Other than Those Which It Receives as a Result of Its Programming.

You do not possess a single bias or belief that arrived with you at birth. But from that moment on, how far you have come! You came into the world with a clean, clear mind, ready to be filled up with everything there was to learn about the wonderful world around you. By the time you were three or four years old, you had already adopted beliefs that would affect you the rest of your life. And by the time you were six, you had cemented in place so many beliefs about your self that many psychologists would say your directions were pretty well fixed.

By the time any of us reaches adulthood, we have stored up and we act out a vast amount of biases, prejudices, conceptions and misconceptions, beliefs and disbeliefs—all of them collected by us, none of them ours to start with, and many of them untrue.

6. **When Faced with Two or More Programs That Are in Conflict with Each Other, the Subconscious Will Attempt to Act on the Program Which Is the Strongest.**

This is the characteristic of the subconscious mind that works in your favor when you want to override an old program that has been working against you. Your subconscious has been accepting your old programs, whether they were true or not, healthy or not, good for you or bad, and it has been acting on them because they were the strongest programs your subconscious had to go on.

Give your mind a *stronger* program, and it will act on the new program in place of the old.

It isn't a matter of asking your subconscious to decide which program it will pursue, it is a matter of which program is *stronger*, the one with more emphasis, more emotion, and more specific direction.

NO MATTER HOW STRONG OR HOW IMPORTANT THE PREVIOUS PROGRAM

Most of us would be surprised to learn how many decisions we make are controlled by the programs which happen to be the strongest programs we have *at the moment*. Strong programs override weaker ones, and the programs that win out, at the moment, play a powerful role in how we think and what we do at the time.

Even in anything as minor as which breakfast cereal you will choose tomorrow morning, to something as important as whether you should quit your job and find another one, the decision you end up making will be the result of those internal influences which are the strongest.

Those influences are affected and controlled by the feelings, attitudes, and beliefs contained in the thousands of programs that fill up the file space in your subconscious mind.

The rule in its simplest form is: *The strongest program wins.* What this means to you as a Self-Manager is that if you want to get the better of something that has been getting the better of you—inside you—you can overpower or override the undesirable program.

If you are dealing with a previous program that is weak, it should not take too strong a new program to override the old one. If you are dealing with past conditioning that is overwhelming, then your new programming must be strong enough to overpower *it*. The subconscious mind will indifferently follow the clearest path. It is up to you to create that path. And you create that path with your Self-Talk.

7. The Strength of the Program Is Influenced by the Number of Times the Same or Similar Information Is Presented.

Your subconscious mind will accept and attempt to act on anything you tell it if you tell it often enough and strongly enough. The more times you are presented with the same information, the greater the likelihood that you will accept it.

This principle is the reason for the *repetition* that we use when we want to create a new Self-Talk program that sticks. Advertisers have known and used this principle of repetition for years. If you were to ask almost anyone living in the United States, over the age of fifty, to finish the sentence "Lucky Strike Green goes to . . .," it's likely that with no thought at all, they would finish the sentence with the word "war." And they would do so automatically, even though that particular advertising line hasn't been used since the end of World War II.

Any child over the age of three or four will quickly point out that "you deserve a break today . . .," and he or she will just as quickly tell you where to go to get it. Whether we *think* we believe it or not, we actually believe that there is one brand of tissue that is more "squeezable" than the other brands. And it is our subconscious minds that are the true battlefields on which the war of the taste tests has been waged.

Whether your external programs come from advertisers, friends, family, or the people you work with, if the programs they are selling are the wrong programs for you, you can choose not to accept them—and replace them with better programs of your own. With a little practice, and the right kind of self-directions, you can decide for your self which choices to make, and implement those choices with self-programming that works in your favor.

You have a great deal more control over your own input than you may have given your self credit for. You can use repetitive self-direction for anything you'd like—and as soon as you realize how it's done, this time the choice is *yours*.

8. The Strength of the Program Is Influenced by the Perceived Importance of the Program Source.

We often say, "My daddy used to tell me . . .," or "My mother used to say . . ." We support our biases with "According to . . .," or "I read it in . . ."

When it comes to Self-Management, the source of the program becomes very important. Your conviction in accepting the information affects the emotional content of the programming process. The result is: The better the *source*, the better the program.

This is true of any programming, any information you receive from any source. But it is especially true in *self*-programming because in Self-Talk *the source is you*.

The more important you make your own Self-Talk, the more effective—as a program—it will become.

All of us, especially when we are young and most impressionable, receive programming now and then from someone else that sticks especially well—possibly even for life.

An example of this is a story I was told of a young boy who was privileged to meet a leader from his parents' church. Shortly after they had been introduced, the church leader said to the boy, "Young man, you have the spirit in you to become one of our church's finest leaders. If you continue as you are now, that is what you will become."

The prophecy proved to be self-fulfilling. The young man

grew up to become the head of one of the largest church denominations in the United States. The boy may have received divine guidance from the "spirit" the elder had talked about, but he was also influenced by something else—a conscious and unconscious program presented to his subconscious mind by someone he greatly admired and respected.

In this case the *source* of the program—the church leader—increased the importance of the program and thereby the *strength* of the program itself. Had the boy heard the same remark about his future from someone he disliked or mistrusted, the outcome might have been far different.

Casual, passive, incidental, and accidental programs play their part in your subconscious conditioning. But specific, conscious, direct programming from a source you believe in creates some of the strongest programs you will ever receive.

9. The Strength of the Program Is Influenced by the Amount of Emotion Associated with the Program.

Your emotions increase the strength of a program *by increasing the amount of electrochemical activity in the brain!*

Events that create emotions get your attention—especially if the emotion is not one that you have worn out from overuse. You will remember the movie you cried at—especially if you are not in the habit of crying at every movie you see. You can recall, as though they all happened yesterday, times when fear froze you in your tracks, a time when you laughed so hard you thought you could not stop, the moment when your nervousness made you wonder if you could get two words of a speech out of your mouth without stumbling.

When you do an ordinary thing in an *extraordinary* way, you remember that event longer. It is something that doesn't fit just right, it is out of place, and your subconscious mind takes special notice; you have more of your senses involved.

For example, imagine sitting at home repeating Self-Talk to your self to create more "energy and enthusiasm." As you will learn, using the right Self-Talk in almost any circumstance, even sitting quietly at home, will create a subconscious program which the brain will begin to work on.

But imagine repeating the same Self-Talk about creating energy and enthusiasm while you run down the beach, wearing a bright yellow swimsuit, and then fling yourself headfirst into the water, after shouting out each set of Self-Talk phrases!

Will your Self-Talk program stick now? You bet it will— probably for the rest of your life. (And everyone who is watching you at the time will probably remember it for the rest of *their* lives, too!)

I'm not suggesting, of course, that you go that far to create a unique programming event, but it becomes easy to see that adding *importance* to the programming process can add *life and emotion* to the program itself. It is also why some of the most effective techniques for using Self-Talk are also the most interesting.

10. The Subconscious Mind Will, at All Times, Attempt to Act on Its Dominant Operative Program.

As in the characteristics discussed in rule #6, which talked about "conflicting programs," this tenet carries the predictable activity of the subconscious one final step further. Whatever you do, for whatever reason you may *think* you are doing it, you are following the *leading* programs in your subconscious mind.

Every behavior you have is influenced by the *strongest* programs you have on file in the program banks of your mind.

ARE YOUR PROGRAMS WORKING FOR YOU?

What you do today, tomorrow, and every day for the rest of your life will be dependent, at least in part, on those programs. You could deny it, overlook it, disbelieve it, or fight it, but the physiological reality of what makes you tick will remain the same.

These rules of the brain and subconscious mind exist for your benefit. They were designed to work on your behalf, helping you to survive—to do *better* than survive. They can even help you reach a part of the potential that we hear so much about *others* reaching.

Guided and directed in the right way, your own mind will help you create a life that works better for you. Making life work better is something that most people hope for.

If achieving that lifelong quest is important to you, then learning to use the one tool that can help you achieve that goal is an essential first step.

SOMETHING WE'D LIKE TO CHANGE

Most of us have a few things about our selves we would like to change. And most of us have found in the past that making changes has often proved to be more difficult than we had hoped. Few of us were taught what it takes to make any *lasting* change work.

Making changes in our selves is not a one-step process or an overnight event. We are not one way one day and another way the next. There is a reason for this: The brain was not *designed* to make sudden, permanent changes.

The brain—with its billions of neurons and its millions of pathways, circuits, and memory cells—does not, in a day, a week, or a moment or two, dismantle its immense network of previous programs, wipe the slate clean, and suddenly replace the old network with a vast new storehouse of different programs. It does not, in the twinkling of an eye, give you a firmer figure, a new attitude about your job, supreme confidence, or a better relationship with your family.

The brain is constructed to follow patterns of habit. It is not constructed to jump frivolously from one behavior pattern to another. When we try to make a major, rapid change

49

in our selves, we are asking the brain to do something it was not designed to do. In fact, if we did not develop strong behavior patterns, our species would not survive—and the brain would not be performing its primary function.

The result is that in most cases our brains resist the change. The weight of previous programming is too heavy to force aside with one big push. That is why change, *true change* in our personalities, in our attitudes, and in our patterned behavior, does not happen often or rapidly.

But just because most of us have been going about trying to make changes in the wrong way doesn't mean that it's impossible to improve. We all know that people do make lasting changes. And all those who do, whether they are aware of it or not, are making the changes *in a way that is natural to the brain's normal operation*. Learning to work *with* the natural processes of the brain is something most of us can do.

Trying to do better is natural to our species. That we *try* is one of the best things that can be said for us. But overall our track record in uplifting our selves has not been very good. A study of our own history tells us that we think, act, achieve, or fail today in just about the same ways as we did when humankind first put chisel to stone and carved out its earliest messages to us.

From the earliest recorded times, we as humans have dreamed, worked, planned, risen, fallen, loved, fought, questioned, and survived. But in all that time, nothing much about *us*—as humans—has changed. We still get up in the morning and face the day in much the same manner as our earliest ancestors faced theirs. We don't have the same problems they did, of course, but with a few changes of props and scenery, the play is still the same.

Though it can be proved that we have changed in physical stature, I doubt that it would be as easy to prove that we have changed in the stature of our minds. We are, in many ways, still as warlike, scrambling, and insecure as the earliest man. We live not far from the campfires of our past.

Pick up a copy of the morning news and you will recognize that in some ways we have not come far at all. In spite of our progress in science and in material well-being, we have not kept pace in our mental and psychic well-being.

Some of the most respected writings regarding our behavior were written by people who lived two or three thousand years ago. Many of those teachings have yet to be improved upon.

In addition to civilization's revered religious works, the words of early writers and philosophers like Socrates, Aristotle, Confucius, Mencius, and Seneca are still regarded as high points in helping us understand human nature.

THE DAWN OF SELF-MANAGEMENT

If you study the planet earth long enough, you might conclude that when it comes to making any improvement in how we think, we will *never* change. There is nothing to prove that, at least as far as modern man is concerned, we have ever changed; so what is there to prove that we will now?

But if you examine our past—and our present—carefully enough, you will find that something is happening right now, something is taking place for the first time—and it is a potentially life-changing event on a broad scale:

Something is taking place—in our lifetime—which has never happened before in the history of mankind: *The mind of man has developed the technology to figure out the mind of man.*

The technology, which we created, is now helping us map *the process of the thoughts* that created the technology in the first place! The human brain is the only mechanism we know of which could possibly figure out the human brain. It has taken us a long time, but we are finally doing it.

The more we learn about how the mind works, the more we learn what its rules are, and how to use those rules to achieve practical, *lasting* change for the better.

In *What to Say When You Talk to Your Self,* I outlined in detail a process called the "Self-Management Sequence." That sequence defines how we arrive at our successes—or failures—as a result of our programming. The sequence works like this: 1. We become *programmed.* 2. Our "programming" creates our *beliefs.* 3. Our "beliefs" determine our *attitudes.* 4. Our "attitudes" create our *feelings.* 5. Our "feelings" determine our *actions.* The end result is that our "actions" determine whether we succeed or fail.

What we do is determined by the programming we receive; if we want to change what happens next, we first have to change our programming.

We have also learned a process by which we can get in step with our own *natural* programming process. It involves not simply *deciding* to make a change, but, instead, *creating, through our own self-directions, a chain of events—steps in the mind—that result in the changes we want to make.*

The changes take place because our brains naturally follow the same mental paths that they follow in adopting ideas and adapting to change—also naturally—*when we are not even aware that the changes are taking place.*

THE THREE STAGES OF
SELF-MANAGEMENT

There are three stages of Self-Management that are natural stages of *change*. Unless you approach these stages consciously, and are fully aware of what you are doing, the steps will happen without *you* taking the time to determine the outcome of what happens *to you.*

The result is that you end up with an old form of Self-Management that is nothing more than "management by *chance.*"

The stages of change have been operating within you all along. They are the normal progression you go through to move from where you *were*—to where you are *headed*. Stage one is where each thought or self-direction starts its journey. Stage two is where you reconsider where you are going, assess your progress, and recheck the map along the way. Stage three is when you arrive at your destination.

If you start by giving your self the right directions, and carefully check your course along the way, you vastly increase your chances of arriving where you want to go.

THERE IS NO BETTER TIME

If you continue to expect your self to make sweeping changes without recognizing that the brain just doesn't work that way, you will be frustrated and unfulfilled—upset with life, quietly angry and not knowing why.

As an individual, it is your own programming that is responsible for making you the way you are and influencing how you live your life, each and every day. It is the programming each of us contains that makes society as a whole the way *it* is.

Up to now, most of our programming has been a mess. Three fourths of our own self-talk is working against us, and unless we do something about it, the situation isn't going to get any better.

Take a look at the results: Behavioral researchers tell us that as much as 60 percent of the work force in the United States say they would like to be doing something else; two thirds of all marriages end in divorce; as many as half of all graduating high-school students have experimented with drugs; alcoholism is at an all-time high; and 30 percent or more of all adults suffer from some form of frequent or chronic depression.

The list goes on much longer than it *should*—and it is much longer than it *would* be if we learned to manage our lives toward achieving the best for ourselves instead of allowing our own questionable programming to manage *us* toward attaining much less. The wrong kinds of subconscious programs—those that create negative results in our lives—have played an ever-present and often negative role in determining how well things work out.

Our own programming has done us an injustice. Because of it we have gotten pretty good at doing things wrong. It is time we started learning how to do things right.

FIRST STEP— "SELF-TALK"

THE FIRST STAGE OF SELF-MANAGEMENT

When you are learning something as important as Self-Management, making a change in your own Self-Talk may seem like a small thing to do, but it is the best way we know to get things in gear.

How you begin—the Self-Talk you start with—will affect and direct all the Self-Management that follows. Your Self-Talk will set your direction, give you a picture of your destination, and encourage and motivate you along the way.

Because Self-Talk is the first and most important step in the Self-Management process, it will help to know what Self-Talk *is* and what Self-Talk is *not*. Here are some of the questions which are asked most often about Self-Talk, along with the answers.

What Is Self-Talk?

Self-Talk is a means of consciously reprogramming your subconscious mind through the use of specifically worded phrases of *self-direction*.

Where Does Our Natural Self-Talk Come From?

None of our self-talk is actually *natural;* we learn most of it from someone else. Unfortunately, because of the number of times we hear the words "no," "cannot," and other forms of negative programming from others, we learn to duplicate the same forms of negative programs in our own self-talk—of which as much as 75 percent is negative or counterproductive and almost entirely unconscious. The implication is that as much as three fourths of the self-programming that we believe is *natural,* is *unconscious,* originates *outside* of us, and works *against* us.

In a sense there are really two kinds of self-talk. The first is the kind that we create, through habit and repetition, for ourselves. The second is the "unconscious" kind that comes back to us, from within, as a result of the first kind. This second form of self-talk is a reflection—*an unconscious repetition*—of the self-talk we have learned to say silently, unknowingly, or out loud.

Is the New Form of Self-Talk a Cure-All?

No. If there were a magic cure for our problems everyone would be using it already. Self-Talk is, however, a psychologically sound method of changing the subconscious programs that affect all behavior—and thereby all change, all failure, and all success. *Self-Talk is a means to an end, not an end in itself.*

What Is the Difference in the Use of the New Form of Self-Talk and the Self-Talk That We Were Raised with and Which We Have Been Using Unconsciously?

First the new Self-Talk is used consciously—which puts us back in control of the most important part of our programming. In time, the new Self-Talk—which we learn—becomes as unconscious or as natural as our old form of unconscious self-talk was in the past.

Does Everyone Use Self-Talk of One Kind or Another?

Everyone talks to him- or herself 100 percent of the time—at least during the waking hours. During that time, each of us carries on an internal dialogue that is mainly subconscious; we are not generally aware of what we are saying to our selves.

Is Our Self-Talk Always Worded in Specific Phrases or Sentences?

Some of our self-talk is worded in sentences, but most of it is not. Most of our unconscious self-talk comes to us in the form of partial thoughts, mental nudges, feelings, intuitions, and simple phrases that are duplicates of previous thoughts.

Can Anyone Learn Self-Talk?

Anyone who uses words to communicate can learn Self-Talk. Even very young children model much of their early programming on what they hear from adults. The use of Self-Talk is universal in that since we all use an unconscious form of self-talk from earliest childhood, anyone can also learn to *modify* his or her self-talk to create mentally healthier self-programs.

The use of Self-Talk is not subject to an individual's background, education, sex, past experience, or present circumstances. The brain accepts Self-Talk because *all* Self-Talk is compatible with the brain's normal programming process.

Is Self-Talk Something You Have to Memorize or Learn Word for Word?

Self-Talk becomes a habit principally through *awareness*—that is, being consciously aware of what you say to your self about anything. However, it does help to repeat certain phrases of Self-Talk to your self often enough that those phrases become automatic models for the rest of your Self-Talk to follow.

Is Self-Talk Recommended for Use with Any Problem Regardless of Its Importance or Severity?

Most problems can be affected or improved by the right kind of Self-Talk. In most instances Self-Talk will either help with the problem itself, or it will directly affect how effectively we *respond* to the problem—and therefore how well we *deal* with it.

It is important to understand, however, that Self-Talk is not designed to work just on problems; it is equally effective in working on goals, attitudes, or other desired changes. When Self-Talk is used in its most effective way—as a *preventative*—the need to use it with problems is less likely to become a necessity.

Is Self-Talk the Same as Old-Fashioned Positive Thinking?

No, it is not. Much of the new Self-Talk is neither positive nor negative—it is simply self-*directed*. For example, your new Self-Talk may direct you to become more aware of being organized or of taking steps to organize something specific such as the paperwork on your desk.

While accomplishing the task may offer "positive" benefits, the Self-Talk itself is neither positive nor negative, by itself, but rather a specific statement of direction that you are giving to your subconscious mind.

The use of Self-Talk should not be confused with earlier concepts of simply maintaining a "positive attitude." The use of Self-Talk is, instead, the application of specific self-directives which are worded in a specific way in order to achieve a predetermined result through the natural processing and response functions of the human brain.

While the concept of Positive Thinking deals primarily with *attitudes* only, Self-Talk deals with the subconscious programming that affects a much *broader* group of behavior modifiers, including *beliefs, attitudes, feelings,* and *actions*.

Is Self-Talk Anything Like So-Called Brainwashing?

No, they are not at all similar in method or in purpose. The use of brainwashing techniques is actually nothing more than a manipulative form of *stress programming* that uses extremes of deprivation and rewards to create a psychological imbalance, a need to become stabilized, and a willingness to cooperate with those who are creating the imbalance.

Self-Talk is precisely the opposite. Self-Talk creates balance and *self*-control. It is healthy, beneficial, self-directed, and is, in fact, a means that can be used to *counteract* external conditioning and control of many kinds.

Is the Use of Self-Talk New?

An early form of spiritually oriented "affirmations" predated the present form of Self-Talk, and the concept itself is very old. However, the use of specific new Self-Talk phrases, repeated in a prescribed way as part of a planned *program* of personal self-development, is a recent breakthrough that is the result of two decades of developments in medical and neurological research and of other conclusions derived from behavioral research.

Is Self-Talk in Its New Form Now in General Use?

Self-Talk concepts have been studied and tested sufficiently in the fields of education, sports, health, etc., for us to understand how the same concepts can be applied to personal day-to-day Self-Talk practice and use.

In the last several years, Self-Talk has been put into practice in medical clinics, therapy centers, drug-rehabilitation programs, school classrooms, business-management programs, weight-loss centers, athletic organizations, and other institutions, as well as being adopted by many private individuals for a variety of uses, including every imaginable area of personal development.

Is Becoming Adept at Using Self-Talk Difficult?

Fortunately, learning Self-Talk is not difficult. The use of Self-Talk follows a process which corresponds to the natural programming function of the human brain. When we use Self-Talk of any kind, we are following and using the exact same programming process which we have used since birth. We have always given our selves self-directions. But when we consciously use the new form of Self-Talk, we are improving the *quality*—and thereby the *result*—of those self-directions.

Self-Talk does require a certain amount of attention, especially at first, but it can be learned by almost anyone. Any child old enough to speak, even in the most basic sentences, can learn to use it.

Will Repeating Self-Talk Phrases a Few Times, or Even Occasionally, Create Permanent Changes?

Absolutely not. Although the use of *any* amount of the right kind of Self-Talk creates some benefit, Self-Talk is not an overnight solution—at least not for achieving long-term changes. It takes more than a few casual attempts at applying Self-Talk to create an automatic habit of using it. On the other hand, you can be sure that if you continue to give your self the same wrong directions contained in your *old* self-talk, you will *not* succeed in creating the changes you are trying to make.

Is It Necessary to Speak Out Loud When You Are Using Self-Talk Phrases?

There are times when repeating Self-Talk phrases out loud can have a very beneficial effect. Most Self-Talk, however, is accomplished silently. Initially you learn it by listening to tapes, by reading, by speaking the phrases out loud, or by repeating them silently. After a short period of time, the new Self-Talk becomes most frequently of the silent type, and not even noticed by the person using it.

Is There More Than One Kind of Self-Talk to Deal with More Than One Kind of Situation?

There are four general categories, or uses, of Self-Talk. These include:

1. *Self-Talk for* Changing Attitudes
2. *Self-Talk for* Internal Motivation

3. *Self-Talk for use in* Solving Problems or Accomplishing Goals

4. Situational Self-Talk *which is used for dealing with situations that are unpleasant but necessary.*

Although all the new forms of Self-Talk are worded in a similar way, the Self-Talk in each of the categories alone is worded specifically to deal with each area individually.

Do You Have to Believe in the Concept of Self-Talk for It to Work?

Because "Self-Talk" is only a name we have applied to a natural process by which the brain collects information and acts on it, the process will continue to work whether you understand it and accept it, or not. You can help the process work *better,* however, by working *at* it; if you understand the process, there is a better chance you will give it your full support.

CREATING THE PATH OF LEAST RESISTANCE

By nature, we tend to follow the path of least resistance. Not only is it human nature, but it is also a neurological fact; the electricity of the mind, like lightning, finds the most direct path to follow.

If you think of *programming* as creating pathways through the computer circuits of the mind, it is easy to see why the stronger programs win out, and why Self-Talk, a very strong form of programming, is so effective in creating the clearest pathways.

By using the right kind of Self-Talk, *you are literally creating a new path of least resistance*. But this time, because you set the direction yourself, the *clearest* path is also the *best* path to follow.

This is why your own Self-Talk is so crucial as a first step in the Self-Management process. The paths you create are the paths you follow; where you end up depends on how you start.

THE BENEFITS BEYOND THE FIRST RESULTS

If using Self-Talk on a regular basis did nothing more than get you moving, encourage you to think differently on a particular day or moment, make you feel better, prop you up when things get you down, create some new belief in your self, change the way you look at problems, get you to set some new goals, or help you stop being so tough on your self—that would be more than enough reason to start practicing Self-Talk today and keep doing it.

But Self-Talk's most important—and lasting—benefits are those which happen down the road, almost as gifts to you from your self that arrive at your door when you least expect them.

When we first began studying the use of Self-Talk in typical day-to-day situations, we did not yet know what the final results would be. An earlier form of Self-Talk technique had been used successfully by athletes, as well as in other areas that require intense concentration and a cool head under extreme stress.

During an Olympic competition, as an example, it was not unusual to see athletes practicing their "athletic Self-Talk"—sometimes out loud—just before their events took place. I remember, when watching Olympic events on television, seeing top athletes go through a Self-Talk warmup as a part of their regular warmup exercises. The television cameras often caught these athletes as they literally *pre*played their upcoming performances—*mentally*—by feeling each muscle move in perfect coordination and giving themselves winning record-setting Self-Talk self-directions as they conditioned themselves for potentially medal-winning events.

Even when Self-Talk was being used to set new records for athletes, it was also beginning to be used by regular people in ordinary circumstances.

We were looking for its effectiveness in on-the-job situations, in dealing with relationships at home and socially, in developing spiritual growth, and in helping people deal with difficult problems like depression, chemical or alcohol dependency, habit control, and weight loss. We were looking for near-term results that could, with reinforcement, turn into longer-term solutions.

We found that the near-term results exceeded our expectations. Self-Talk was more than holding its own as a significant tool for effecting short-term internal motivation and change.

But Self-Talk also created positive results in a variety of other circumstances. It proved to be universally effective not only in the number of areas in which it could be used, but also in the wide variety of people who could take advantage of it.

It was sometime later, however, after the first Self-Talk had been put into general use, that we were able to assess Self-Talk's *longer*-term results. What we found was not only encouraging, it was exciting. Self-Talk proved to create *secondary* benefits, after the fact—after it had helped individuals overcome the initial problems or situations they were dealing with.

The results that people were experiencing weeks and months after they had first used Self-Talk also indicated that they were directly related to the specific new Self-Talk they had started using. In many instances an individual would use Self-Talk for a period of time, and then stop after he or she was satisfied that the initial problem no longer existed. But even after the Self-Talk was put aside, it appeared that the subconscious mind was still using it—*on its own*.

Here was a clear case of individuals creating new program paths in the brain, and then, without being aware of the next step in the process, stepping aside and letting the brain take over and unconsciously *continue the same form of self-direction their Self-Talk had started!*

THE FIRST STEP IS UP TO YOU

Once started, the process from Self-Talk to *Self-Management* becomes self-generating. If you start off in the right way, you will continue to move through the second stage and on toward the third stage automatically. That makes the first step all the more important, but it also tells you that if you take the time to get started right, the rest of the way should be easy—like taking more new steps, but down the same path—and in a sense it is.

As you will learn in the following chapters, what happens after you get started happens almost in spite of you.

The first step is designed to help you set a new direction and then get out of your way; stop interfering with your own progress. It is the *next* step—the second stage of Self-Management—that will show you whether you took the *right* first step.

YOU'LL KNOW WHEN IT'S WORKING

THE SECOND STAGE OF SELF-MANAGEMENT

After you begin using Self-Talk, if you stay with it for a short period of time, even three or four weeks, you will begin to move into the second stage of the Self-Management process. This stage is one of the most interesting parts of the journey.

It is in stage two that your subconscious mind begins to *assimilate,* or digest and absorb, the new programming. Let's say, for example, that you have learned to change some of your old self-talk, which was working against you, to new Self-Talk, which is worded to help you see your self in a better light.

An example of old self-talk might be: *"I never seem to get anyplace on time,"* or *"Nothing ever works right for me,"* or *"I hate to even think about going on this interview."*

Instead of continuing to replay your old programs, you

have now learned to give your self new self-directions: *"I am always on time"; "Things are working right for me. I'm in control and I'm doing better than ever"*; or *"I'm looking forward to the interview. I know I'll do well!"*

It is after you have actively begun to use your new Self-Talk that stage two begins. It is in this stage that a battle is silently waged, with the new words of Self-Talk pitting themselves against the old. It is also in this stage that you begin to feel and experience the first of the long-range benefits of Self-Talk.

TYPICAL BEGINNINGS

A friend of mine decided to try Self-Talk to reach the simple goal of getting more exercise. Using the cassette method, Dave began by listening to Self-Talk for Exercising two or three times a day for two weeks.

During the first day or so, Dave did not see any noticeable change in his exercise habits—or in his thinking. Sometime during the third or fourth day, however, during a conversation with a friend, Dave caught himself just as he was about to say, "I get started exercising, but I never seem to stay with it." Instead, he found himself saying, *"I look forward to exercising nowadays."* As simple as that comment was, the change surprised him.

By the end of the second week, Dave was still exercising, and he noticed he was starting to feel different about exercising. He even found himself looking forward to it! He was hearing the right words, getting the right encouragement, and he noticed that the things he was telling himself and saying to others were sounding more and more like the Self-Talk he was practicing. He also noticed that the Self-Talk was beginning to sound more *natural*—as though the *new* person he was describing to himself each day was actually *him*.

I mentioned earlier that the use of Self-Talk is a means to an end and not an end in itself. If Dave had stopped after just two weeks of Self-Talking, it would likely have been because he did not understand the real goal—the much larger and worthwhile *end result of Self-Talk*.

By using Self-Talk, my friend exercised. However, by starting the *habit* of Self-Talk, Dave created something more.

THE MEANS TO AN END

By itself, the instant motivation of Self-Talk is great. In fact, there are many people who start out using Self-Talk for that one benefit alone, never expecting anything more, and not even realizing that the real benefits are yet to come.

If you are like most people, when you begin using Self-Talk you will enjoy the internal motivation that it will give you. Take advantage of the great new supercoach inside of you, letting you know that you *can* do it. Allow your Self-Talk to relax you or keep you moving. Use it to focus your attention, look at problems and opportunities differently, and begin to look at your *self* differently.

But don't forget that that's just the first stage of building a new Self-Management team within your self. Those benefits are the first results; usually they are the first to be noticed, and the first to let you know that there may be something to this self-direction business after all. But you are just getting started. There's more in store.

WHEN YOUR SELF-TALK IS WORKING

How do you know when the process is working? What are the signs that tell you that you are on the right track?

During stage two of the Self-Management process, if you want to judge your progress it will help if you know what to look for. *If your Self-Talk is working,* here is what you can expect:

1. Your Old Programs Will Argue to Keep Their Place in Your Mind.

During a period of time after you begin using Self-Talk, you will find your self—your *old* programs—questioning the new information you are giving yourself. You may even notice a kind of *internal argument* going on—with *you* right in the middle—between the old programming and the new.

It is at this time that you begin to see the emergence of a "new self." This new self is not a product of wishful thinking; it is a very real part of you. It is that part of you which challenges the old self and says, "I have decided to make this change in my life. I'm determined to make the change, and you'd better listen to what I have to say." The "old self"—the old programming—doesn't want to hear that. If your new Self-Talk is working, if it is getting through, your old programs that you have been carrying with you will fight to stay in control. When that happens, don't worry about it, enjoy it! It means your new Self-Talk is working.

It is exciting to realize that each of us, every day, has the right and the opportunity to create the beginning of a new self and to challenge the old self that we no longer choose to accept.

When you use a new kind of Self-Talk, you begin to give your self some completely new descriptions of who you are. You are handing your subconscious mind a new picture of at least a part of you, and saying, *"This* is me—not that other person I *thought* was me all this time."

Let's say that you have begun using Self-Talk to get more things done on time, to stop procrastinating. So you start by using Self-Talk that tells you, in the present tense, as though you had already accomplished your goal, that you are in complete control of your time. Your new Self-Talk tells you such things as *"I do everything I need to do when I need to do it"*—a good example of effective Self-Talk.

Of course, when we first begin giving our selves the new program, we have not yet become the way we are telling our selves we *choose to become.* But we know that we are *capable of becoming that way*—and we are in the process of making the change.

When we do this we are redefining—for the subconscious mind—who we *really* are, first inside and then, with practice, on the outside as well. *But our old programming does not want to agree.* It says, *"No you don't! You can't make the change. You won't stop procrastinating. Why even try?"* It has worked hard to keep us believing in our old limitations—the ones that caused the problem, and in this example, kept us procrastinating in the first place.

Since when you use the new Self-Talk, you are following a very basic and natural process of the human brain, *the potential for making a change is clearly on your side;* if you keep using the new programming to override the old programming, you will win out.

The more we give our selves the right kind of self-directions, the clearer will be the new paths we are creating in our minds—and the greater the chance that we will begin to follow those new paths automatically. In the example we just used, that means we will begin to see our selves as getting things done on time rather than continuing to put things off. *The way we see our selves most determines what we do most*.

Your old program does not *want* you to change. It will do anything it can to *stop* you. And what it can chiefly do is put up the best possible argument against self-direction, and get you back to being your old comfortable self.

When you begin to use Self-Talk, and you hear your old programs try to convince you that the new programs *can't possibly work*, just smile and give your self a pat on the back. This is a sure sign your subconscious is listening, and your new Self-Talk is starting to work.

2. You Will Notice New Self-Talk of Your Own Making Cropping Up in Other Areas of Your Life.

While the old programs still argue to be heard, you will also begin to hear another kind of internal conversation in areas that may be completely unrelated to the problem or goal that your conscious Self-Talk is working on. For instance, you may be Self-Talking about shedding twenty pounds and suddenly hear your self using a similar kind of Self-Talk for being a better parent, or becoming a better listener, or being more assertive, or for working on some other goal.

In stage two of the Self-Management process, the concept of using Self-Talk begins to branch out *internally*. Because you have been using a new form of self-direction, specifically to get the attention of your subconscious control center, that control center will first sit up and take notice. Then it will begin to apply that self-programming to *other* areas of your life. Why? Because you are now clearing mental paths which are easier to follow. The self-directing system in the mind is designed to function best when it is *repeating* itself—duplicating what worked best last—and applying what it learned to what it has to do *next*.

The result is one of the most lasting benefits of using Self-Talk. When you notice that you are using the new form of self-direction in different ways—some of which have nothing to do with the Self-Talk you started out with—you have reached another major signpost that lets you know you are headed in the right direction.

In time, the original Self-Talk phrases will become much less important than the secondary benefits they create.

3. You Will Start to Notice a Difference in the Way You Talk to Others.

I often hear from parents who say that the *first* thing they noticed about their own change in Self-Talk was that the way they talked to their children had changed. This is true also when you begin to talk to other people—even to someone for whom you may *not* have had a kind word in the past.

Part of the reason for this change is that the new Self-Talk makes us aware of our own self-programming—and at the same time we begin to realize the effect that *our* words can have on others. But there is another reason that is just as instrumental in why, during stage two, we begin to monitor and edit what we say to someone else.

The more we learn about our subconscious minds and begin to understand *why we do what we do*, the more we begin to realize why other people are doing what *they* do—why their attitude isn't always the best, why they get into trouble or make mistakes, why they are sometimes inconsiderate or uncaring, have habits that work against them, or personalities that make them difficult to deal with. *They were programmed, too!*

Coming to that realization about others instills in us a new appreciation of the word "forgiveness." How can we possibly judge other people when their conditioning and their force-fed self-talk has kept them at odds with themselves? I have met many people who, since discovering the implications of their programming and self-*mis*direction, have found new meaning in the words, "There, but for the grace of God, go I."

Using directional Self-Talk leads to a better understanding of *others*. When that happens, those others often begin to respond in kind—they notice the difference in you and may even begin to give *you* the benefit of the doubt.

People have told me that just making the one small change to being more understanding of others would, by itself, make the effort they put into changing their self-talk worthwhile.

4. You Will Become Increasingly Aware of the Old Form of Self-Talk Being Used by Others Around You.

One of the surest signs that your new Self-Talk is working is when you start noticing the amount of *bad* programming other people are using. When you hear it, you may be tempted to correct it. But unless you are dealing with someone in your own family who has already become familiar with Self-Talk, I suggest caution in correcting other people's self-talk—they may not understand and probably won't appreciate it.

What usually happens, however, is that anytime you hear someone else using a particularly misdirecting phrase of the wrong kind of self-talk, it will reinforce your own determination to continue using the *right* kind of Self-Talk yourself.

5. You Will Begin to See the First Evidence of Positive Results.

During even the first few weeks of practicing Self-Talk, most people notice some changes in their thinking—and in their behavior—that they can clearly attribute to their new Self-Talk. In some areas these success signals begin to show up almost immediately; in other areas they take longer.

Self-Talk for becoming a better listener, improving concentration, or being mentally alert typically produces rapid results, sometimes even during the first day or two of practice. But getting over a problem of self-esteem, for example, or becoming more outgoing socially will take longer.

During stage two, however, enough changes begin to show that if you have stayed with the process up to that point, you will be anxious to keep going. The longer you continue, the more you are reprogramming your control center to respond to and look for *more of the same*. That is why the old saying is scientifically correct: Your successes create more success.

6. You Will, from Time to Time, Be Tempted to Go Back to an Old Way of Thinking That Did Not Expect as Much of You.

Even with encouraging positive results along the way, now and then we will recognize that we may have bitten off quite a chunk. After all, the less we expect of our selves, the less chance we will have to fail. That isn't *true,* but it *is* logical. *Who wants to try to be perfect anyway?* This is also not realistic, since proper Self-Talk is *never* based on becoming "perfect," but the thought *seems* to be very logical.

There are times when your old programming, the discouragement of people or circumstances around you, and the size of the hill in front of you, all make it seem useless to try to become any better than you are.

When that happens, when you find your self balancing on the fence, unsure whether to work harder or to stop, take heart! If you weren't making progress, your new self-directions would not still be struggling to take control!

While you are aware of what is happening on the surface during stage two, there is much more going on underneath that you are not aware of. During this same time the subconscious mind is busy *adjusting* to the new programming. When you begin letting your subconscious know that you mean business, it will begin taking action on putting the new programs into motion.

MORE IS HAPPENING THAN MEETS THE EYE—OR THE EAR

First, your mind begins sorting through the old files to see what fits and what doesn't, trying to figure out what to make of all this new input. Next, it will start looking for more information to *support* the new Self-Talk, and it assesses and evaluates how it should affect or modify what you should do next. At the same time, your brain will begin creating physiological responses to the new commands, adjusting your electrochemical controls accordingly, and monitoring the results.

Remember that the human brain is designed to help us function at our best. If it weren't, we would not have been given the inborn inclination for "doing better" in the first place. Striving to do better is part and parcel of the biological equipment we are all born with. Even at times when things aren't going right, most of us know within our selves that for some reason we are "set up" to succeed, not to fail.

Fortunately, when the brain begins to sort through the new Self-Talk commands, all this complex under-the-surface activity doesn't concern us since most of it is entirely unconscious and automatic. And if we are using the right self-directions, everything is taking place for our *benefit;* our minds and our brains are doing their utmost to follow the new directions to the letter.

CHALLENGES AND REWARDS

When you begin taking responsibility for directing your self, the end result is always worth the effort. But effort *is* required; there are rewards, but there are also challenges.

One of the challenges is that during stage two, you hear your own doubts coming back at you; you question whether the change is worth it, or whether you are capable of making the change. This is a time when you may have to come to grips with how you really feel about taking responsibility for your self—for your thoughts, for your actions, and for your own future.

Stage two is also a time when a part of your direction will be undecided, out of balance. You may want to make the change but feel unsure, inadequate, or unready to deal with having to make a commitment to your self and see it through.

But then there are the rewards. Stage two is a time of a new sense of *self,* a reawakening of dreams and watching them begin to take form both before you and within you. It is a *confirmation,* a nod of benediction from your *higher* self, a recognition that you are letting more of the best of your self develop and grow. It is the beginning of freedom from old shackles, and the first step from skeptical disbelief to confident self-acceptance.

Among these initial rewards is a willingness to see yourself in a way that you may not have for many years: You are less daunted by the obstacles and more enthusiastically compelled by the rewards.

That requires, of course, that you take the first step and stay with it so that the second stage can begin. When you do, you will have the first few reins of control back in your hands. You will be leaving less to chance, little to luck, and nothing to wishful thinking.

If you are looking for instant success, you will not find it here. If you are hoping to find a mythical pot of gold waiting just for you at the end of some rainbow, there is none. If you would like to look into a mirror tomorrow and witness a miraculous overnight transformation, you will see that nothing is done with mirrors. What you will find, instead, is a reasonable, workable solution; one that is natural and one that you can count on.

STAGE TWO IS THE NATURAL RESULT OF STAGE ONE

In stage one (changing your Self-Talk) you begin the process of reprogramming by changing the specific directions you give to your self. While you are using the actual Self-Talk phrases, you experience direct results—most of them temporary. But you are setting the wheels in motion.

In stage two these new self-directions begin to create a chain reaction of responses.

As you internalize your Self-Talk, your subconscious mind reviews it, processes it, tests it, and begins to expand it to areas other than those with which the Self-Talk deals directly. The subconscious mind, which by now is beginning to recognize the new pattern of directions, starts to duplicate the same kinds of directions without your having consciously to direct each of them.

Eventually the pattern grows. What was only a short time ago a collection of Self-Talk phrases which you listened to, read, or repeated to your self, has now begun to set a pattern for other thoughts to follow. The process which *you* started *has started to grow on its own.*

The more you continue to give your self new self-directions, the more the process expands, takes root, and slowly but surely begins to force the old programs of misdirections aside. *For you, the idea of taking personal responsibility for your self has just moved from a* concept *to a way of life.*

TEN

THE END RESULTS OF SELF-DIRECTION

THE FINAL OBJECTIVE—THE THIRD STAGE OF SELF-MANAGEMENT

The first stage of managing your self takes only days. The second stage can be measured in weeks or months. But the effects, the *benefits* that occur in the third stage of Self-Management, last for years. Now, let us see what is waiting for you when you reach your destination.

The true benefits of Self-Management are seldom found on a list of goals or objectives—although any of them would qualify as the worthiest of goals. These benefits are the *freedoms* which Self-Management creates—the unshackling which frees us from the limitations we have lived with in the past. It is these freedoms which are the *real* benefits that Self-Management brings to our lives:

1. The Freedom of Personal Responsibility

When it comes right down to it, you are the only person who is really responsible for *you*. And the only way you can ever take full control of your own responsibility for your self is by *managing* your *self*.

Everything you ever do, every action you ever take is affected by how much *responsibility* you take for your self. You can wait and let the world take responsibility for you (it *won't*) or you can find a way to take that task on yourself naturally and effectively.

We are fortunate. We have learned that accepting personal responsibility is a natural result of managing our selves. It is a gift that we receive whether we bargained for it or not.

Next to self-esteem, taking full responsibility for your own thoughts and actions is at the very core of your success as an individual. Even when a child decides to finish his homework before going out to play or watching television, he is taking personal responsibility for himself. He has learned that it is up to him, not someone else, to be responsible for his success in school.

The woman who makes sure that her personal apparel projects the appropriate image for a business presentation she is making, is taking personal responsibility, not only for her appearance, but for an important aspect of her career.

The man who decides to come home and help his son with a scouting project, instead of working late at the office, is exercising his freedom to take personal responsibility for *his* choices in life.

Personal responsibility is essential to all worthwhile achievements, all accomplishments of lasting value in your life. And it is a freedom that is a benefit of managing your self.

2. The Freedom of Independence

We seldom do anything well—for or with anyone else—unless we are first standing solidly on our own two feet.

When we were young, we learned to lean. We needed others to prop our selves up on—and they were there, at least some of the time, when we needed them. But as we grow older, as maturity sets in—along with the beginnings of self-sufficiency—one by one, the props are taken away.

If we then allow others to step in and give us new props, direct our lives *for* us, we tie our selves to a life of being dependent on others—never fully standing on our own, never fully allowing our selves to be counted or counted on. When we learn to manage our selves, we learn to stand on our own—not remote or indifferent, but capable, independent, and reliable.

Constructive independence, the self-standing stability of a well-managed self, creates in us the bedrock of self-confidence and self-assurance. It is the strength of our independence that allows us to share with others, to support, to need, and to fulfill. Rather than causing us to stand apart and distant from life, it is our *independence* which gives us the freedom to embrace it.

3. The Freedom of Self-Control

Imagine being so on top of things that you did the things you knew you should, but were not unduly tempted to do the things you shouldn't. That is a benefit of managing your self. Self-*control* is what keeps us in balance, feeling right about things and good about our selves.

It is our control over our own selves which gives us the qualities we cherish as *human.* The freedom of self-control gives us dominance over habits and fears that once made us servants to their demands. It is self-control which allows us to carry our thoughts, our emotions, and our actions safely in our own hands, with no one else having to control *us.*

A corporate executive once told me that his decision to learn self-control had given him the freedom to stop smoking, to balance his household budget for the first time in years, and to make positive changes in the way he got along with his wife and children. He had been "successful" in the past, but before he found the freedom of self-control, he had not really found the happiness he was looking for.

The freedom of self-control is a by-product of Self-Management. And it is *essential* to a life well lived.

4. The Freedom to Choose

By managing our thoughts we manage our minds—and by managing our minds we give our selves the freedom to choose.

We are often faced with "choices" in which we feel we have no choice at all. On the road through life we sometimes feel as though we were on a travel tour—with all the destinations already set by somebody else. But when we Self-Manage, we play a far more important role in both determining our destination and in making even the smallest decisions along the way.

The freedom to choose goes beyond, for example, the decision to say yes or no to the peer pressure a young person may experience when being offered drugs or an opportunity to take a wrong path. The woman who chooses to give herself a day of free time, away from the demands of job and family, is exercising her freedom to create balance and wellness in her life. Most of the people I talk to who have learned to make choices in their lives—and stick to them—tell me that they had wanted to make those decisions all along, but in the past they hadn't felt they were entitled to make them!

You have the right to say yes to choices which make life better, happier, and more productive each and every day. You have the right to say no to choices that create unhappiness or unhealthiness in your life.

The management of your self gives you the insight and the freedom to make good choices. And making good choices is the affirmation of a healthy, active, Self-Managed mind.

5. The Freedom to Change

We often meet an opportunity to make a change in our lives—a change we would *like* to make—only to find that our old programming has different ideas. It is like coming to a railroad crossing where we stop, look, and listen, but never get up the courage to cross the tracks.

So many people have told me that they felt stuck in their lives; they couldn't change jobs or careers, couldn't change personal relationships, weren't able to change their weight or appearance, or couldn't change the financial "level" that they believed life had handed to them.

Freedom to change is permission to stop getting in your own way. It is permission to do what needs to be done to make your life more the way you would like it to be—and that includes making changes in some of the smallest details of your daily life.

Freedom to change is freedom to grow—it is your own *approval from* your self *to* your self—and it is the most important approval you will ever receive.

6. The Freedom to Fail

I remember the story of the electronic researchers who were perfecting the movements of a computer-controlled robot by letting it bump into the walls going down a hallway, correct itself, and move on until eventually it had *learned* how to roll down the hall by itself.

We humans tend to look at "bumping into walls" as *mistakes*, even though we learn in much the same way as the robot was learning. To the robot's technicians, those bumps were not mistakes at all; they were nothing more than re-quirements for midcourse corrections.

I cannot recall a single biography of an individual who achieved success and fulfillment in life without failing—usu-ally several times—along the way. Without the stories of their *failures*, most biographies would be thin books with few pages.

There is no shame in failing in the process of working at doing your best. Freedom to fail is the freedom to *learn;* it is the freedom to falter—without losing sight of the goal.

When you become a Self-Manager, you give your self the freedom and the confidence to fail. That is your *right*—and it is an essential ingredient in your success.

7. The Freedom to Succeed

In an employment interview, a friend of mine was asked the question "Are you open to success?" For a seemingly simple question with a seemingly obvious answer, I suspect responses to it were more telling than most of the applicants knew: We are very often *not* open to success.

So often we are programmed to believe that success will not happen, or that we are not capable of reaching it, or that someone else will reach it instead of us, or that we don't really deserve it. Sometimes, too, we accept some other equally inaccurate program that tells us that, for some false reason, we will not, or cannot, be as successful as we ought to be.

But that is our *old* programming—the kind of programming that guides us *before* we become Self-Managers. To succeed in anything, we must first give our selves the freedom to succeed.

A number of books have been written about how some people subvert or sabotage their potential successes. I have talked with scores of hopeful weight losers, for example, who told me that each time they got within ounces of their goal, something happened and they put all the weight back on again.

Have you ever known someone who failed in his work or business because he stopped short of his goal—*just when the goal was finally in sight?*

When I ask individuals such as these to give me examples of the kind of self-talk they have been giving themselves, I usually hear self-talk statements that are clearly designed to *force* them to fail.

Why do they do it? They do it because they have never known that, no matter what earlier programming they may have learned, if they want to break through the "success barrier" and finally succeed, first they have to *re*program within themselves the natural acceptance of success.

That acceptance is often sadly lacking in much of the programming that we carry with us into our adult lives. Have you ever heard someone say about somebody, "He is his own worst enemy"? Most of us, in many small or sometimes important ways, could say the same about our selves.

When you learn to manage your self, you learn to *accept* your successes—not avoid them or subvert them. To Self-Managers, successes become a natural extension of self-direction.

8. The Freedom to Deserve

For many of us, our past programming has included some strong admonitions about what we deserve and what we *do not* deserve from life. In the past, when it came to believing that we deserved the best, for any number of reasons the "do nots" all too often won out.

I received a letter from a woman who for many years had wanted to operate a business of her own. But even her family, including her parents, were against it. During those years, she had frequently found opportunities to start a business for herself, but she had never taken the step.

"I was convinced I could not do it because I believed I did not deserve to make that kind of move," she wrote. "None of the things that independence and owning my own business could give me were on my list of things I thought I deserved."

It was only through finally retraining her own subconscious attitudes about herself that the woman realized she *deserved* whatever she decided to create in her life, and she finally reached her goal. She quit her job as a salesperson with a large national electronics firm and started a company that made accessory items for the same industry she had worked in. Changing how she looked at what she *deserved* from life brought her to the realization that she had every *right* to succeed as a businesswoman—and her successful business today is living proof that she had *deserved* to achieve her goals all along. Until she readjusted her self-belief, by reprogramming herself to *deserve*, she had unknowingly held herself back from achieving her own, well-deserved success.

You cannot reach any height you do not *believe* you *deserve* to reach. When you manage your mind, you open your self to accepting what you deserve freely and fully; you recognize that the successes you experience are the natural results of your efforts.

Self-Management gives you the freedom to see your self as worthy and deserving, to be willing to accept your responsibilities and meet your opportunities, and to enjoy the rewards they create in your life.

9. The Freedom of Truth

In your old programming, when it came to assessing who you were, or what you were really capable of, many of your choices were *not* to select the options that were the truest. *"Truth," with careless programming, is often masked, and looks like something else entirely.*

How could you tell what was true when your old programming was doing such a good job of hiding it from you? How could you know what was true in any area of your life when you did not have the programming to know what was true about *you?*

How can a boy ever believe that one day he *could* pitch a no-hitter in the World Series when he has learned to believe that he has little or no chance of even making it as a second-rate ballplayer on a farm team? Imagine the self-talk that he would, in time and with enough discouragement, learn to use on himself. More than likely, that boy will never recognize that the "truth" he *accepted* about himself may not have been *true* at all.

Some of the most important truths you could ever hope to find in your life are those which you learn to believe about your self. And yet, unless you learn to accept the *real* truths about your self, how can you possibly expect to live up to the best of the self that you *could* have been?

When you become a Self-Manager, the truth about your self and others becomes the *reality* you choose to accept. Self-Management gives you the direction to recognize the *real* truth about who you are, what you are capable of becoming, and how to make the best of your self work with the world around you.

10. The Freedom of Self-Esteem

Strong self-esteem is not only a result of Self-Management, it is an exceptional gift from *you* to your *self.* If there were no other benefits from learning to manage your self, a healthy self-esteem would by itself make any price paid for Self-Management worthwhile.

Once again, by becoming a Self-Manager, you increase your good fortune. Self-esteem comes with the territory. And it is a gift that surpasses any other wealth of mind you could ever hope to attain.

TO LOVE YOUR SELF IS TO LIVE AT YOUR BEST

There is no other facet of your self that plays a greater role in your life than your own individual *self-esteem*. It is the *lack* of self-esteem that is found somewhere at the root of most of the problems we have with our selves, most of the problems we create for others, and in every failure to reach our better potential.

A *healthy* self-esteem, on the other hand, creates confidence, consideration for others, and a worthwhile, productive, well-balanced life.

Self-esteem is so fundamental to our complete well-being that it stands apart from, and above, every other ingredient in the nature of man—with the possible exception of divine spirit itself.

The freedom of self-esteem is a natural result of Self-Management. When you understand what self-esteem is, and the role that it plays in your health and in your life, you begin to understand that the only thing that could be wrong with self-esteem is not having enough of it. Self-esteem is, and will always be, one of the most helpful and most necessary parts of who you are.

When you give your self the freedoms that Self-Management creates in your life, you learn some new things about your self. But can you overdo it? Can you really *believe* this exciting new self that you are creating with your own self-direction? We are about to find out.

ELEVEN

ARE YOU KIDDING YOUR SELF?

When for many years you have been giving your self one kind of self-direction, and then you suddenly begin to give your self new directions that may be just the opposite, are you telling your self the truth?

If, for instance, your old programming told you that you were not an organized person, does suddenly giving your self a new program that says you are now an "organized person" mean that you are kidding your self—telling your self something about you that is not *true?*

Or perhaps for years you believed that you had trouble getting up in front of a group and speaking comfortably. Your old self-talk was saying, *"I get nervous every time I have to speak in front of a group."* But now you learn to say instead, *"I enjoy speaking to people. When I speak to a group I am confident and relaxed."* Which is true—your *old* programming or the *new?*

A friend of mine told her self for twelve years that she wanted to stop smoking, but that she couldn't seem to quit. Then, using specifically worded Self-Talk, she began a Self-Talk program that told her that she was a nonsmoker. Was she telling her self the truth? (Yes. She became a non-smoker.)

It is true that the subconscious mind accepts what it is told, if it is told often enough and strongly enough. But is it true when you first start telling your self that it is? How can we be honest and still give our selves *new* programs that clearly contradict the old?

A NEW TRUTH IN TRANSITION

When you begin to give your self new self-directions, you are beginning the *process* of creating a new truth about your self. However, the day you begin your new Self-Talk, you have not *yet* reached the goal; you are not *yet* the new person you are describing your self to be.

But you are not kidding your self. What you are really saying is *"This is the way I CHOOSE to be."* Your conscious mind *knows* you haven't done it yet. It knows you are *working at* fixing the problem. Give it time! The subconscious mind will begin to accept the new direction as true—and do everything it can to make it happen.

Your new Self-Talk is replacing or overriding an old program *that was not true in the first place*. You are not kidding your self now—*you were kidding your self when you accepted the old false program to begin with*.

As we have seen, we were not *born* with our beliefs and our biases—we acquired them. We learned to believe that we were shy, or not organized, or not creative, or that we could not make enough money, or that we avoided problems—or any of the other countless *"truths"* about our selves that were never true at all.

CHANGE THE WORDS TO MEET YOUR NEEDS

If it bothers you to tell your self future truths in the present tense—such as *"I am good at keeping my finances in order"; "I am never affected by the negative opinions of others"; "I have no problem keeping my weight where I want it to be";* or *"I have no habits which injure my health"*—

whatever it is that your Self-Talk is working on, change the words but keep them in the present tense.

Those same Self-Talk examples can just as easily be said this way: *"I choose to be good at keeping my finances in order"; "The person I am becoming is never affected by the negative opinions of others"; "I prefer to have no problem keeping my weight where I want it to be; I have made the decision to have no habits which injure my health."*

YOUR SELF-TALK IS THE NEW BLUEPRINT OF YOU THAT YOU ARE GIVING TO YOUR SELF

When an architect submits a completed blueprint for a new building, he does not hand over an incomplete sketch of a partially finished building; he gives the contractor a precise picture of every detail of the construction. That is what we are doing when we give our selves a new self-direction in the present tense. If we word our Self-Talk in vague descriptions of hoped-for events, our subconscious minds will not get a clear picture and will not act on it.

Since our subconscious minds act on those programs that are the strongest, we do our selves a favor by delivering self-directions that are simple, direct, clear, and *complete*.

Decide what changes or improvements you want to make in your own architecture—the picture of the self that you would really like to be—and give that description, as completely as possible, to your subconscious mind.

We have been told for years that we should *visualize* the goal, see it clearly in our minds. But we now have a way to do that even if we have not been successful in the past at creating those visual blueprints.

Our own Self-Talk creates the words that create the *visual* pictures for us. All *we* have to do is begin by creating the right words. When we do, the internal picture of the goal follows naturally.

GOING FOR PRACTICAL POSSIBILITIES

Because our own self-believed limitations have held us back in the past, in our zeal to make the change, we may want to break through the fence of our old limits with a bulldozer instead of opening the gate in the fence and walking quietly through.

When we first start using Self-Talk, some of us set our sights too *high;* we forget that the changes we make have to be practical and realistic. On the other hand, others of us listen too closely to our old programming. We never try going through the fence at all, and end up falling short of any real change because we set our sights too *low.*

It is for this reason that I recommend that you begin using the new Self-Talk to fix one problem at a time, or reach one practical new goal. Give your self some time; work first at getting into the *habit* of talking to your self in the new way. Get a few small successes under your belt, and then go for more.

Even if you are reading this book because you want to deal with a *major* situation in your life, when you first start using Self-Talk, do your best to work on one small problem or one goal at a time. *If you ask too much of your self, too little is what you will get.* Keep your Self-Talk realistic. Most of us know when we are asking the impossible of our selves. And most of us know when we are making it too easy on our selves by demanding too little.

CAN THE EGO GET TOO GRAND?

Can you, by giving your self a new picture of the "better" you, develop a picture that is too good? Can you give your self too much self-esteem?

The process of overriding past programming and building your self up *could* seem like "self-praise." One question I have been asked is "What about being 'boastful'? *Could my new Self-Talk end up overdoing it?*" As one young mother asked me, "If my son hears all these good things about himself, won't he think he's *too* good?"

Perhaps the *wrong* kind of self-talk could create that belief—but *never* the kind of Self-Talk we are discussing here.

People who begin using Self-Talk do hear, often for the first time, some very nice or wonderful things about themselves. But instead of the new Self-Talk phrases creating a false sense of ego or a "better-than-the-others" attitude, they create a *stronger* appreciation for *other* people while they build an increased appreciation for one's self.

The new Self-Talk does not attempt to put you above others—or make you think you are better than you should be. On the contrary, it helps you pull your self up to where you belong, and gives you the caring and compassion to help *others* reach their heights as well.

When we see someone whose sense of self seems grossly inflated, we tend to think that that person's ego has gotten out of hand. We think that he or she is conceited or vain.

But what we are really witnessing in such a case is not the result of a *strong* sense of self at all. We are seeing just the *opposite*. The most frequent cause of conceit, vanity, false pride, or arrogance is a *lack* of self-esteem, or a lack of self-worth.

Too *little* self-esteem, not too much of it, makes us compensate for what we feel we lack.

KEEP YOUR SELF-TALK IN BALANCE

Remember that Self-Talk is just *the first step in a process* that leads you away from an old way of thinking and doing things to a natural new way that is better for you. You are not trying to build monuments to your self. You are not trying to make vast changes in a few days. You cannot; that just isn't the way you're made.

Your success at Self-Talk will have a lot to do with how well you keep your self in balance—and that means setting your sights on practical goals, and giving your self the kind of Self-Talk it will take to reach those goals.

Most of us have more wisdom than we give our selves credit for. When we try to tell our selves that we can do the impossible, we know that we are not being completely fair with our selves. When we hear our selves say inside, *"I can't"* when it comes to something we should tackle, we suspect that we *might* succeed.

There is something in all of us that senses what we can

accomplish and what we cannot. Our past programming will usually try to convince us that we cannot. But that "something," which is part of the human spirit, has also been trying to convince us that we can do better. Listen to the inner part of you that tells you, *"This is for me. I can do it."* With a little practice you will know the difference between telling your self what is *potentially true* about you and what is not.

I have known people who, with the right use of self-direction, have created changes and benefits in their lives that seemed unattainable on the day they began. I have watched young people in their teens who have learned to like themselves in ways that changed their whole perspective of who they were. They have learned to keep from doing poorly in school or from going along with schoolmates who try to convince them that it's okay to experiment with drugs.

I receive letters daily from people with realistic goals who have applied their self-direction to marital problems, or to learning to be more responsible, to making changes in their careers, or to overcoming obstacles which they had previously believed were insurmountable.

These are real people, just like you and me, who have had personal problems and objectives of every imaginable kind—and who came out on top because they began to understand the incredible effect of adding their new *truth* to their own self-programming. When they began to talk to themselves in a better way, they were not kidding themselves at all. And they proved it.

The more you practice, the more you will find that each time you set your goals, and use the right Self-Talk to help you achieve them, your objectives will slowly but surely move higher and higher from one goal to the next. In time, the real *truths* about your self may prove to be exactly those things you *thought* you were kidding your self about when you first started using your new Self-Talk.

YOUR NEW SELF-TALK IS THE REBIRTH OF THE REAL TRUTH OF YOUR SELF

We are frequently the *least* truthful with our selves when we continue to accept the negative programming from our past. Yet we continue to give new life to our old beliefs, long after we should have thrown them out and replaced them with new beliefs that are more helpful and more honest.

When you use appropriate, practical Self-Talk—in which you see your self in a better, healthier, more successful new way—*you are not kidding your self.* You are finally setting the record straight.

TWELVE

OVERCOMING PROBLEMS FROM THE PAST

During my years of exploring the field of self-directed behavior, I often considered the following questions: "Does Self-Talk deal with the problems of our past without covering them up? What about the problems that have such a hold on us that they *need* to be sorted out and dealt with?"

What about your past? If you want to change your future, do you first have to go back and relive your past problems so you can sort them out, understand them, and get rid of them? Can you solve your problems (or change your future) by what you do *now* without *first* fixing what you did about problems in the past?

Your own Self-Talk should not attempt to replace any other practical therapy or approach that helps you solve problems or look at life in a more productive way. If you are using counseling or other therapy, *if it is working for you, stay with it!*

Self-Talk deals with a different side of your psychological anatomy. It deals with the side which encourages you to take *personal* responsibility for who you are and how you handle your life.

We have *all* had problems in the past. Some of us were tested more than others. Some of us went through what seemed like unbearable psychological hardships. At one time or another, *most of us* thought we would not make it.

And so we struggle with the past and we say, "But *this* happened to *me*." And sometimes we let the past upset the present—because we cannot let go of it.

Many people tell me that they have problems today because of something that happened in the past—sometimes years ago—an unhappy childhood, an abusive parent, the loss of a mother or father, an early mistake that got them into trouble, or a failed marriage.

When you are not willing to let go of what you endured in the past, are you really being *fair* to your self? Most of us have had traumatic experiences that would paralyze us if we gave them half a chance. Some of us even continue to relive those early traumas and failings as though they were happening to us today.

RE-CREATING PROBLEMS OF THE PAST GIVES THEM NEW ENERGY IN OUR SUBCONSCIOUS MINDS

Until recently, many of us accepted the hurtful memories of past problems without considering what a profound effect *reliving* them had on our subconscious minds. We did not understand one of the basic tenets of the subconscious: *The human brain does not know the difference between a real experience and an experience that is created or re-created in the mind*.

Instead of "Does your new self-direction ignore past problems?" the question should be "*Do you want to create more electrochemical (mental) energy to re-create the same perceived experience over again in your mind*—and re-program the same bad experience one more time?"

We all have the ability either to dwell on the past or move past it and go forward. I am not suggesting that it is easy to get past the past. There are lessons in all our pasts that have helped us grow stronger. But eventually everyone has to move on. I often recall the adage "You can't get where you're going when you're looking in the rearview mirror." What is past is past. What is ahead of us is *clearly* ahead of us—if we will just give it a chance.

If you have had problems in the past, even severe ones, you are not alone. Some of us could write a book about what went wrong. Few of us have escaped the pitfalls which were a part of our learning. Some people move past them and move on. Other people dwell on them, give them more energy, re-create them, and allow them to stop them cold.

LIVING IN THE PAST

I talked to a woman recently who was very depressed. When I asked her why she was so unhappy, she recounted a list of things that had happened to her in the past. She had suffered a divorce. Her son had become involved with drugs, and on several occasions had attempted to end his life. She had been forced to find a job and start a new career entirely on her own.

Every problem the woman spoke of was of utmost importance and had a great impact on her life. But all the problems she discussed had taken place several years in the past—and she was still living every one of them!

As a guest on a television program, I was asked to answer questions from viewers who had been invited to call in with their problems. I remember in particular a young man who called in to say that he was unable to find work. He felt his life had come to the end of the line. His wife had left him several years ago, and he had gotten involved with the wrong crowd.

He told me, and the other television viewers, that all of his problems started when he was fired from a job for stealing electrical wiring from a contractor he was working for. Because of that incident, which had happened seven years previously, the man told me that he was convinced nothing he did would work out right.

Over the years I have heard many true, and emotionally strong, *negative* stories. I have listened with interest and concern, but I have also learned to understand the effects that the self-imposed continuation of *past* history can have on our *future* history. Not all of the stories I have heard turned out bad.

I know of one woman who spent thirty years of her life fighting her problems, based on an emotionally abused childhood. All throughout her youth and adult life she had wanted to become a writer, but her past and continuing problems convinced her that she could never become the author she had one day hoped to be. Her unhappy childhood and teenage years had left her with deep emotional scars that stayed with her, often causing her to *relive* the pain as though it were happening again.

But I saw this same woman learn to accept her past, and eventually put it behind her. I watched her life change as she turned it around and became a successful writer. She went on to use her past experiences to create beautiful stories of hope and vision, and share them with the rest of the world.

I remember talking with a young man who, simply because of the incredibly negative experiences he had had as a child, should have been rendered almost helpless as an adult, but went on instead to become a world-class computer whiz. I have a friend who grew up in a broken home, had to battle his way home from school every day, and felt he was *destined* to fail. But because he decided to forget the *bad* and go with the *good,* he has made a fortune in electronics.

For every story we know of someone who was determined to hang on to the past, there are many more stories of people who said, "Enough!" and got down to the business of moving ahead instead of looking back.

When you learn about the natural processes of the human mind, to continue believing that "you can't have a good future because you had a bad past" is no longer an acceptable excuse. Feeling good about having climbed the mountains of past adversities is healthy—but *dwelling* on the failures of our own past inadequacies only makes things worse.

INSTEAD OF RELIVING YOUR PAST— *PRELIVE* YOUR FUTURE

None of us has been completely safe from the growing pains of our past. And *all* of us have a future in front of us.

How do you want to live the future that you have in front of *you?* Do you want to live the rest of your life rehashing the inequities, the unfair events in your past, or would you rather start right now to get where you would like to go?

You have probably heard the statement, "Be careful what you want out of life—you will probably get it." When I first heard this years ago, I thought it made sense, but I did not know at the time that this old saying would one day have scientific support.

It is your choice to look backward and live with the fears and problems of your past, or to look forward—with exactly the same amount of electrical input to the mind—and help create the circumstances of your future.

When you arrive at the future, it will not be luck that got you there. An uncanny amount of it will depend on how well you do at letting go of some of the failings of your past, and go about addressing some of the better opportunities that lie ahead of you—*if* you are willing to bite the bullet and start creating them for your self, *now.*

YESTERDAY IS GONE—TOMORROW YOU HAVE A CHOICE

Tomorrow is an option. For most people, because they do not understand how much control they *could* have, the future will be left to *chance.* For them, tomorrow will prove to be as regular and as average, as bewildering and as confounding as today is, and every day that went before. There is no direction for what lies ahead; they will only struggle to get by and deal with tomorrow as best they can. That is how they have dealt with *tomorrow* in the past; that is how they are destined to deal with tomorrow in the future.

For those who are dwelling in the past, the future will be another rerun of an old movie, written with an uninspired script, with predictable old scenes, played on an endless loop of fading film, to the same tired audience, and with only the same trite ending in sight.

For those who are moving *forward* in life, tomorrow may bring the exciting option of new possibilities, well-laid plans, and untried beginnings. For them tomorrow is worth waking up for. It is only if you have overcome your past that you will be able to feel the radiance of tomorrow's sun. Learn from the past, and put it behind you. The new man and the new woman are born each day.

You *can* overcome the problems which you carry from your past. The best way, if a problem is not too overwhelming, is to let it remain a part of the past and to get on with your future. Life, we are told by those who have lived it, is very short. It makes sense to make the best of it, not the worst. If you have problems from the past that nag you, leave them where they belong—in the past.

It makes no sense to recharge your brain with old electricity—re-energize old programs to rekindle old fears and give new life to old pain. There may be some old business that was never taken care of and needs tending to, but if there is something from your past that you know you should deal with, *deal with it*—and then close the file on it and address your mental chemistry to something else.

None of us can undo what has already been done. But any of us, if we choose, can look past the past, set our sights on the future, and start changing things now.

The past should, as has been said, bury the past. We have enough to do just getting ready for tomorrow.

THIRTEEN

WHEN *YOU'RE* NOT THE PROBLEM

Let's assume that in a short while you will have fixed your own Self-Talk and are actively trying to make things work better for you. Now what do you do when your own life and your own Self-Talk are great—but other people whom you have to deal with have the same old kind of self-talk? When you begin changing your own self-directions, you may as well get used to no longer thinking like most people think.

Have you ever had to deal with someone whom you felt you could not accept or tolerate? Most of us have been in situations where we have had to put up with someone like that, and felt there was nothing we could do about it. Sometimes it's a person who lives with you. Or, it's someone you work for—a teacher at school, or a friend whose attitude may make you wonder from time to time if that person is really a friend at all.

For you, as a self-directed Self-Talker, the appropriate way to deal with the problems others sometimes create for you is to decide now to *be prepared* for those problems before any more of them come up.

You cannot take responsibility for another person's actions, but you *can* take responsibility for everything *you* add to the situation. You already know in advance that you're not likely to change the other person—nor is it your right to do so.

RECOGNIZING SELF-TALK PROBLEMS IN OTHERS

When you deal with someone who is a problem to you, you can improve the way you handle the situation by recognizing the *conditioning* that is behind the other person. You are dealing with that person's past programming—and his or her own form of self-talk, good or bad.

When you get angry with someone, are you really angry with *him*? Or if you think about it, aren't you really reacting to the *results* of his programming? The next time you are confronted with a situation that could get you upset and thinking negatively about your self, ask your self three questions:

> **Question 1**—*Is the problem a result of the other person's programming?*
>
> **Question 2**—*If the problem comes from the other person's programming, can I really do anything about it?*
>
> **Question 3**—*Is my own programming contributing to the problem?*

The next time someone says or does anything that would have upset you or caused a problem for you in the past, immediately ask your self, *"Is it their programming? Can I help? Or is it me?"* By asking questions like these you quickly become aware of how often you may have allowed someone to upset you, when in fact it was the other person's negative conditioning that created the breakdown in the first place, and perhaps your own negative reaction that added fuel to the fire.

This does not mean that when someone treats you badly

or does something that is clearly out of line, you should immediately smile and say, "I forgive you for being the way you are—after all, you can't help it." (If you started doing that, you would lose a lot of friends fast or make a lot of enemies quickly!) But the ability to forgive is always preceded by the ability to *accept*.

The fact that you become aware of the other person's programming does not make that person "good." It does not right the wrong. It does not change the other person's path through life; he may not even be aware that you have decided to accept him. But when you recognize that the other person has his *own* files full of old programs that he lives with, you will respond to him differently.

When you do this, you are not suddenly trying to change the way you act with everyone around you—nor are you trying to make every relationship perfect. You are making a small but very important change in how you treat others. Repeated often enough, that change can create days and weeks and months and, in time, a future of better relationships for you.

It is your responsibility to be in control of what you think and how you feel. This includes how you feel when someone is inconsiderate, argumentative, insensitive, or indifferent, or fails in any way to treat you in the way you think you ought to be treated.

You can choose to respond with the same negative attitude and show the person that you also know how to behave poorly—which will not help either of you—or you can recognize that *the situation is the way it is because of a huge amount of programming that took place in that person—and in you—in the past*.

None of that programming originally had anything directly to do with the present problem, but a lot of it may be affecting it in the worst possible way.

A friend of mine, who had been practicing Self-Talk for some time, told me that he had learned to use a helpful phrase of "instant" Self-Talk whenever a problem arose that was caused by someone else's conditioning: *"When in doubt, back off, settle down, lighten up, and reconsider."* If you and the other person—whom you feel has the problem—were completely to reverse roles, and at the same time exchange each other's past programming, you can be sure that some of your thinking would change—fast!

For many years therapists have taught people how to practice trading roles with another person, especially in a close relationship. Their teachings are designed to help you learn to be more understanding of other people's feelings and points of view. You can learn the positive effects of those techniques very quickly, the next time the opportunity arises. Ask your self the three questions outlined above. And for just a moment, pause—and listen to your answers.

WARDING OFF THE NEGATIVES OF OTHERS

There are times when the situation is tough enough, and one-sided enough, that the best thing you can do is to protect your own "good" attitude from being influenced by the "*bad*" attitude of the other person.

You may feel at times like you have suddenly stepped in front of a target, and somebody is holding a bow and a full quiver of arrows. What you tell your self at that moment will determine whether the arrows, if they come your way, will hit the mark or not. It is your *mind* that the arrows are aimed at. It is your own Self-Talk that will either throw them to the side or let them hit home.

You have probably experienced times when someone has had a bad day, and you happen to be the one that the other person takes his frustrations out on. I sometimes wonder how many arguments that take place at home after work really happen because of wounded or sensitive attitudes that were built up during the day and which had nothing to do with two people arguing.

Negative energy thrown your way packs more punch because it is charged with emotion—and emotional input creates stronger programming. Don't let those emotions hit the target. Ward them off with your own Self-Talk.

When you choose to fight someone else's negative programming, you are doing battle with negative energies. If you choose to fight back, by responding out loud to the person, or with silent thoughts to your self, you are only creating more anger, more anxiety, more stress and unhealthiness in your self.

Arm your self instead with clear, simple Self-Talk statements that direct your own mind to let no harmful, unwise, or unkind thoughts step in and take hold. Stay in touch with who you *really* are. Give your self the directions that build inner peace—in spite of the turmoil that may be going on outside of you.

When you do this, you are not ignoring the other person or the problem. In the past when people told you simply to *ignore* someone's attitudes or words, they failed to take into account that unless you replace the negative input with something else, the negatives would come rushing in anyway. They have to be overridden, replaced with something better.

Tell your self, *"I alone am responsible for what I think. The negative thoughts from someone else only serve to remind me of my own winning healthiness—and I always feel good about my self."* Or say to your self, *"This too shall pass, and nothing that this person is saying to me can harm me in any way."*

And it never hurts to add, *"I understand—he has programming of his own. It may not be the best, but it is the only programming he has."* That's not belittling the other person or putting him down. It just means *you* consciously recognize that he is doing no more than acting out the programming that directs his life.

The more you become accustomed to using Self-Talk in many different situations in your life, the more that kind of Self-Talk will automatically step in when the situation needs some extra help.

DEALING WITH ATTITUDES THAT ARE "DOWN"

Not all the problems you encounter with others have to do with people saying the "wrong" things or treating you badly; it is simply the *attitudes* themselves that are difficult to deal with.

At times, a person, especially someone who is close to you, may exhibit an attitude that is "down," or depressed—

generally negative—and if you do not keep your self in check, you can begin a *negative cycle* within your self.

It works like this: You first try to get the other person's attitude to change. It doesn't change, so you become frustrated, and your frustration soon turns to low-level anger, which grows. The angrier you get, the more the other person's attitude bothers you. And now the negative cycle is off and running.

Have you ever known someone who affected you that way? It is a tough cycle to get out of. Unless you or the other person does something about it, matters will continue to get worse until the relationship breaks down completely. Or the problem will stay with you like an old pot of tasteless soup, simmering over a low fire on the back burner, stirred up and brought to a boil now and then by an argument or a few cross words.

If someone else's attitude bothers you, you might as well decide right now that it is up to *you* to stop the cycle. If the other person's attitude is bad enough, it is unlikely that his own conditioning—in its present state—is going to help him do anything to fix the problem by himself.

What you *can* do something about is *your* attitude—and you can do it now. You have the ability and all the equipment necessary to protect your self from a negative cycle by refusing to be a part of it. You do not have to say a word about it to the other person. Just step out of the cycle; get out of its way. When you do, it will lose its energy.

MAKE SURE THAT *YOU* ARE NOT THE REAL PROBLEM

There are times when the *real* problem is simply that you are at odds with someone because he is not doing what *you* want him to do.

When you are learning how to self-direct your own life in the *right* way, you will begin to recognize that no one has the right to try to live another person's life for him. You do not have the right to choose to change other people just to suit *you*. For your own reasons, you may want the other person to change. But it is up to others to make their *own* choices themselves.

Some people stay in trouble with everyone around them simply because they are trying to take responsibility for everyone else's behavior and never for theirs.

Take a look at your relationships with the people in your life—long-term, short-term, or even momentary. If the real problem is that other people refuse to act or behave or think in a way that you would like them to just to suit *you,* then you already know what to do next. Stop it. Stop trying to change other people to suit your own needs. Allow them their full right to take responsibility for their own choices in life. *This does not mean that you should relinquish your responsibility to help others.* But there is an important difference between *helping* others and trying to live their lives for them.

The basis of all Self-Management is learning to take responsibility for our selves. *Why would we ever want to stop someone else from having that same right?*

Instead of spending your energy converting someone else to seeing things *your* way—spend it on dealing with your *own* responsibilities. If you have been trying in any way to take away someone else's responsibility for his life, you may even want to apologize to that person. It will make both of you feel better—and it will let you know that, as a *self*-manager, you are on the right track after all.

Part of your success as an individual will always depend on how well you handle your relationships with other people. In your relationships your own Self-Talk will play a role of exceptional importance. What you learn to say to your self in any circumstance, in any problem with any relationship, will always *affect the outcome of that relationship.*

As in so many other important areas of our lives, we all have a great deal of control over the outcome of our relationships—*regardless of who may have had the problem in the first place*. What you and I choose to do with our *own* Self-Talk will be the deciding factor in what works and what doesn't.

FOURTEEN

WHAT WE'VE LEARNED ABOUT LEARNING SELF-TALK

Self-Talk has been practiced and learned by many people of almost every age and background. And we have discovered that there are simple steps or methods that make Self-Talk easier to learn. It is from other people just like us, who have already tested and practiced Self-Talk, that we have learned what works best.

The first step to learning Self-Talk is to set just one goal—to begin with, change just *one* habit. Instead of trying to tackle too many goals at once, it is a better idea to set your sights on one objective that is readily attainable, something you are sure you can achieve. In this case, we have learned that the best *first* objective is to create the goal of learning the *habit* of using Self-Talk—first consciously, then, in time, unconsciously as well.

CREATING A NEW "MANAGER HABIT"

One of the most important primary habits is called the *"manager habit,"* which creates or *manages* the *rest* of your habits. Manager habits aren't the kind you use to manage someone else; they are the habits you use to manage your *self*. It is the development of this one manager habit—in this case your habit of using Self-Talk—which leads to changing *other* habits, changing *bad* habits into *good* habits, and creating other new habits of your own choosing.

Your manager habits are your internal supervisors—they direct and affect all of the other habits you have. This is why you can work so hard at times to change one kind of behavior or another, only to find you are slipping back into your old habits.

In this case the problem is that you didn't change the more powerful *manager* habit that controlled the lesser habit you were working on. Your manager habit says, "I'm still the boss," and when it comes to habits, the manager habit always wins.

WE LIVE THE RESULTS OF THE HABITS WE CREATE

The goals you reach are the results of the habits you learn. If you have set goals in the past and haven't reached them, one of two things has been wrong: Either the goal was unrealistic, or the *wrong* habits kept you from reaching it— and the *right* habits weren't there to keep you moving.

I have known people who learned *about* Self-Talk, and immediately wanted to jump into getting the *results* of using Self-Talk. They wanted immediately to change every major and minor habit or problem in their lives, and tackle every goal they had ever had. Even though they had become familiar with *why* Self-Talk works, they were not successful in making the changes they wanted to make.

FIRST OBJECTIVE: CREATE THE HABIT OF USING SELF-TALK

Taking one step at a time is good advice in any endeavor, but it is especially true when you are beginning to use Self-Talk. If you are reading this book to achieve some specific purpose, some goal you have set, you already know what your objective is—but that objective should be the *second* goal that you set, not the first.

Your *first* objective should be simply to begin using Self-Talk, and to continue using it long enough and in the right way so that it becomes a habit—one of the *manager habits* that create the other habits that will affect everything else you do. If you accomplish that all-important primary step, your other goals will not only be easier to accomplish, they may actually prove to be *possible*.

WHEN LEARNING SELF-TALK, CONSCIOUS REPETITION IS THE KEY

I have been asked if it is necessary to *memorize* Self-Talk in order to learn how to use it or put it into practice. It is not necessary actually to memorize specific Self-Talk phrases. Some people, with not-too-fond memories of their school days, would rather do anything than have to memorize one more line of anything.

But although it *can help,* memorizing Self-Talk is not essential to its success. If it were, I suspect that few of us would take the time ever to become competent Self-Talkers. You will find, however, that some of your Self-Talk will lodge itself firmly in your conscious memory banks anyway—whether you try to memorize it or not.

Beyond memorizing a few well-chosen words of Self-Talk as a substitute for reprogramming, which by itself does not work, there are other methods that sound simple enough but are equally ineffective. I have been amazed at the number of "life-changing" solutions we are offered which require no work—no personal investment—in taking the time to do it right.

CONSCIOUS PROGRAMMING IS THE STRONGEST

Scarcely a radio talk show goes by that I am not asked if we can change our programming with the use of "subliminal learning."

So-called subliminal programming—the technique of effortless, "unconscious reprogramming" by using cassette

tapes of quietly whispered, hidden messages of self-direction—is, both psychologically and physiologically, one of the
least effective methods I know to change one's self.

Regardless of what the proponents of subliminal programming would have you believe, the human brain does not
take action on hidden whispers—*it acts on the strongest,
most emphatic, energy-filled program you can give it*. If
subliminal programming worked, it would be an easy way to
get the job done. *But that is not how the brain operates.*

The chemistry of the brain was designed to act on its
dominant—*strongest*—programs, *not* on so-called silent programs or inaudible whispers. That means if you want your
new programs to win out, you have to get the attention of
both the conscious and the subconscious minds *in the
strongest possible way*.

The key to self-programming is **conscious** *repetition;* not
unconscious, vague, or hidden programs, but solid, new conscious self-directions. If you would like to start changing
your programming, your own Self-Talk, you will have to *take
charge*. No subliminal tape or message, no matter how often
the hidden message is repeated, will do it *for* you.

If you want to change your own self-direction, you will
have to do it for your self. If you would like to work the way
the brain works, there are more practical steps you can take.

LISTEN TO YOUR OWN *UNCONSCIOUS* SELF-TALK

During the next days or weeks, anytime you hear your
self making a negative statement *to* your self, or *about* your
self, take note of what you just said—you may even want to
write it down.

Tomorrow morning, for example, while struggling to get
out of bed if you catch your self saying, "I really hate to get
up today," listen to your words, whether said out loud or
silently, and jot them down. If when you are caught in traffic,
you find your self saying something like "I'm going to be late
again," make a note of it. Listen to what you say when a
problem comes up; listen to what you say about anything and
everything throughout the day. Anything you hear your self
saying to your self, or to someone else, that sounds like it

might be a negative self-direction, listen to the words, see them for what they are, and write them down.

After three weeks of learning to listen to your Self-Talk, if you have been faithfully recording your negative self-directions, you should have a small collection of the kind of self-talk that you have used in the past.

The reason for listening attentively to your self is to help you become more aware of what lies beneath the surface of your *conscious* self-talk. As we learned earlier, any single self-talk statement of the wrong kind that we catch our selves saying is just one of literally thousands of similar misdirections that are actively working in our subconscious minds.

PRACTICING A SELF-TALK SCRIPT

The best way to get into the habit of using the right words is to use a practice script—a group of Self-Talk phrases such as those in Part II of this book—that deals with one specific goal you would like to accomplish.

If you are just starting to use Self-Talk, select a script that is important to you. This will be your first complete Self-Talk practice script, and you will be living with it for the next few weeks; you should get to know it well.

When you use this first script, you won't just be practicing *how* to use Self-Talk, you will be letting your subconscious mind practice working on the new Self-Talk at the same time. One of the most widely used techniques is to write the Self-Talk phrases—either taken from this book or similar phrases you write for your self—on index cards.

For the next several weeks, these Self-Talk pocket cards should become some of your closest friends. Carry them with you in your pocket or purse, in the car when you are driving, and keep them next to you on the bedside table at night.

CHANGE "I AM . . ." TO "YOU ARE . . ."

All of the Self-Talk phrases included in Part II of this book are written as individual sets or groups of statements, written in the "first person"—that is, they use the "*I am . . .*" form of statement. When you practice Self-Talk statements, it is also a good idea at times to change the words "*I am . . .*" to the words "*You are . . .*".

For example, a typical group of Self-Talk statements from Part II reads: "*I think clearly. I am organized. I am in control of my self and everything about me. I take responsibility for ME!*"

Your subconscious mind will also accept those words, but in a slightly different way, if you repeat the same statements but change the "*I*" to "*You.*" The same Self-Talk would then sound like this: "*You think clearly. You are organized. You are in control of your self and everything about you. You take responsibility for YOU!*"

The reason for repeating Self-Talk that is both "from" your self ("*I*") and "to" your self ("*You*") is that we respond differently to information which is told to us by someone else. We tend to accept the motivating or encouraging words of a strong coach, for example, because it helps fill our need for outside approval.

When you talk to your self as though an outside person were talking to you, you literally become your own "coach" or motivator, talking to your self just as if someone else were giving you the approval and the encouragement.

The Self-Talk cassettes that I recorded for publication use both the "*I am . . .*" and the "*You are . . .*" form of Self-Talk. On the tapes the individual groups of Self-Talk phrases are first repeated in the first person three times each, consecutively. Then, after all the individual statements have been repeated, the entire group of fifteen or so Self-Talk phrases is repeated twice—once with the "*I*," then with the "*You*" in the third person.

Here is how the original Self-Talk looks and is repeated the first time around. As an example, we will use the Building Self-Esteem Self-Talk script found on pages 148 to 149 in Part II:

Building Self-Esteem

I really am very special. I like who I am and I feel good about my self.

Although I always work to improve my self and I get better every day, I like who I am today. And tomorrow, when I'm even better still, I'll like my self THEN, too.

It's true that there really is no one else like me in the entire world. There was never another me before, and there will never be another me again!

I am unique—from the top of my head to the bottom of my feet. In some ways, I may look and act and sound like some others—but I am not them. I am me.

I wanted to be somebody—and now I know I am. I would rather be me than anyone else in the world.

I like how I feel, and I like how I think, and I like how I do things. I approve of me, and I approve of who I am.

I have many beautiful qualities about me. I have talents and skills and abilities. I even have talents that I don't know about yet. And I am discovering new talents inside my self all the time.

I am positive! I am confident! I radiate good things! If you look closely, you can even see a glow around me.

I am full of life. I like life and I'm glad to be alive. I am a very special person, living at a very special time.

I am intelligent. My mind is quick and alert and clever and fun. I think good thoughts, and my mind makes things work right for me.

I have a lot of energy and enthusiasm and vitality!

I am exciting, and I am really enjoying being me. I like to be around other people, and other people like to be around me. People like to hear what I have to say and know what I have to think.

*I smile a lot. I am happy on the inside and I am
happy on the outside.*

*I appreciate all the blessings I have, and the
things that I learn, and all the things I'll be learning
today and tomorrow and forever—just as long as I
am.*

*I am warm, and sincere, and honest, and gen-
uine! I am all of these things and more. And all
these things are me! I like who I am and I'm glad to
be me.*

Those are excellent Self-Talk statements—all true or
potentially true for anyone who reads them, listens to them,
and makes them a permanent part of his or her internal
program. Now select a few of the same Self-Talk statements,
change the *"I"* to *"You,"* and read them as though you were
actually listening to someone else talking to you.

If possible, read this group of Self-Talk phrases out loud,
preferably while you're looking at yourself in a mirror. *Read
it rapidly and forcefully.* It is one of your new "motivational
pep talks" from you to your self!

*You really are very special! It's true that there
really is no one else like you in the entire world.
There was never another you before, and there will
never be another you again! You have many beautiful qualities about you. You have talents and skills
and abilities. You even have talents that you don't
know about yet.*

*You are positive! You are confident! You radi-
ate good things! You are a very special person,
living at a very special time. You are intelligent.
Your mind is quick and alert and clever and fun.
You think good thoughts, and your mind makes
things work right for you. You have a lot of energy
and enthusiasm and vitality!*

*You like to be around other people, and other
people like to be around you. People like to hear
what you have to say and know what you have to*

think. You are warm, and sincere, and honest, and
genuine! You are all of these things and more. And
all these things are you!

That is one of my favorite forms of Self-Talk. It is the kind of Self-Talk that can be inspiring and uplifting—especially when you read it out loud, or listen to it on tape on days when things haven't been going just right and you could use a good dose of encouragement. And even though it is Self-Talk, from you to you, sometimes these are exactly the kinds of words that other people you care about might like to hear about *them,* too.

READ—OR LISTEN—TO
YOUR SELF-TALK

When you are first learning Self-Talk, or even as you continue to use it later, you may want to use a cassette player as part of the process.

Although all of the Self-Talk scripts included in this book are available as studio-recorded cassettes, you—or a friend—can record any of the same Self-Talk phrases or scripts on a home cassette recorder.

Each prerecorded cassette version of the Self-Talk scripts comes with a set of printed Self-Talk cards. If you choose to record your own tapes, write out each of those Self-Talk phrases on a card—one Self-Talk phrase to a card—to use along with your cassette tape, or to read when you are not able to listen to the tape.

Of course, as simple as it is to get started learning Self-Talk, it will not happen all by itself. I recall the time a man told me that the cassette tapes which he had wanted to use to help him lose weight had not been working for him. When I asked him to tell me how he had been using the tapes—the time of day he used them, how often he listened to them, etc.—his answer was "Well, to tell you the truth, I really haven't gotten around to listening to them yet."

No cassette tape, or this book or any other, will ever do anyone any good sitting on a shelf—other than to remind us what we could have done, and should have done, had we just taken the time, made the decision, and gotten started.

A REGULAR PART OF YOUR
REGULAR DAY

The most effective way to become accustomed to Self-Talk is to make it a *regular* part of each day. As an example, each morning during the first several weeks, and any time afterward when you feel you need some reinforcement, read each of your Self-Talk statements out loud or silently, repeating each statement three consecutive times before going on to the next statement, or listen to your tape completely through once or twice each morning.

Follow the same routine at night, preferably just before you go to sleep.

Do your best to stay with a daily "diet" of Self-Talk *for at least three or four weeks*—and longer, if it is not yet starting to come naturally to you. There is a good reason for this. We have learned that it takes a *minimum* period of time for the subconscious to work through its filing system and redirect us with its *new* program solidly in place.

The length of time will vary from program to program and from individual to individual. The time it takes for your own Self-Talk to start becoming a habit will depend on you and the situation you are dealing with—you will know if you are giving your self too little or too much time to accept the new program and act on it.

This period of time is important. Your diligence in repeating your Self-Talk script at least once each morning and once each night is also important—especially when you are first getting started.

Some people find that they enjoy the "startup" program so much the first time they follow it, that, as soon as the first program is completed, they immediately select more Self-Talk phrases and begin another program. This startup method can be used at any time, for any reason. It allows a massive amount of new self-direction to reach both the *conscious* and the *subconscious* minds simultaneously.

WHEN AND WHERE TO PRACTICE

Self-Talk, in one of its many forms, can be practiced almost anywhere, at any time. But to get into the habit of using Self-Talk, you will have to create the opportunity to practice it. If you get into a routine of using it each day, there is a better chance that you will stay with it long enough for it to start working.

Some of the most effective times and places for practicing Self-Talk are:

1. *The first thing in the morning*

2. *Driving in the car or when commuting*

3. *During exercise*

4. *Walking, jogging, or bicycling*

5. *During meditation*

6. *During rest or relaxation*

7. *In a group at home, at work, at school, or at church*

8. *Just before going to sleep at night*

Whenever, or however, you find it most appropriate to practice your Self-Talk each day, recognize the importance of repetition. Don't be like the man who said he wasn't reaching his goal because he hadn't gotten started. If you want it to work for you, if you want to reach the first objective of Self-Talk becoming a habit for you, you have to work at it.

ONE OF THE MOST IMPORTANT MANAGER HABITS YOU WILL EVER CREATE

Each time you practice Self-Talk, you are creating a new manager habit which one day—in not too long a time—will take over and pursue the goal *on its own*. The purpose of learning Self-Talk as a *habit* is so that in time, your own Self-Talk becomes natural and automatic—a normal part of the way you think and direct your self.

Because Self-Talk creates one of the strongest manager habits you will ever have, *it will affect, direct, create, or control every other habit that is a part of you.*

In a previous chapter, we discussed several characteristics, or tenets, which *manage* the subconscious mind. One of them was: *The strength of the program is influenced by the number of times the same or similar information is presented*.

That's why we practice Self-Talk. That's why we start feeling how it fits for those first few weeks. We are giving our selves a place to begin. To change our other habits or move in new directions, we first have to change the *habit* of programming our selves with our past self-talk—in the wrong way.

Once we learn the *habit* of Self-Talk in the right way, we begin to change the old programs that were overriding and controlling not only our other habits, but everything else about us.

A LIFETIME GOAL

It takes more than a few short weeks to change the programs of a lifetime. But if you want to make the change, the day-in, day-out practice of using the right kind of Self-Talk will get you started in the right direction.

Listen to your own self-talk. Write it down, or make a mental note of it. Then turn it around. Choose a Self-Talk script that applies and begin using it. Obtain one of the professionally recorded Self-Talk cassettes which are available in stores, or make your own. Write out Self-Talk for your self. Become aware of everything you are saying to your self now, and fix it.

For many people, the practice of self-direction will become a lifelong goal. The idea of taking responsibility for their self-direction, every day of their lives, becomes exciting and worthwhile. For people who want to get the best out of their lives, a few weeks of beginning to learn how to talk to themselves will be one of the smallest steps they take.

Once you begin to practice Self-Talk, you may find, as many others have, that your first step—the first weeks or months of practicing and applying self-direction in your own life—was nothing more than the opening of a door. If you continue after the first few weeks of getting started, what lies beyond the door is an exciting new look at your own future, and a very real, practical solution for making it work.

If you were to ask me, "If I really wanted to get what I want out of life, what is the *one* thing I could do?" my answer would be simple. Before I recommend that you set goals, study biographies of successful people, or read popular theories of self-improvement, I would suggest that you *begin* with the management of your *self*.

I would ask you to read these last few pages that show some ways in which to start using Self-Talk, and do what they suggest. And when you had finished, after three or four weeks, I would suggest that you do it again.

FIFTEEN

THE SELF-TALK IN YOUR HOME

It is interesting how often Self-Talk is first practiced by just one member of a family, and within a short period of time the other members of the family are also using Self-Talk. Many letters I receive tell me about someone, usually the father or the mother of a family, who started out using Self-Talk for some purpose that had nothing to do with their home life, and how the entire family ended up being Self-Talkers.

The interesting thing that comes through in most of these letters is that the rest of the family members tend to adopt Self-Talk without any extra encouragement on the part of the person who began to use it first. When you see someone close to you getting control of his life you naturally want to find out more about what he is doing.

I know of families who now have regular Self-Talk sessions. These families sit together, read Self-Talk out loud, listen to Self-Talk tapes, and write out and discuss their Self-Talk and what it is doing for each of them. These sessions can turn into great family and individual goal-setting sessions. When a family is using and discussing Self-Talk as a group, it learns to recognize better personal habits and traits and how to build better self-esteem.

Most of us could benefit by having this kind of attitude-building Self-Talk, and the unity it creates in our homes. We all benefit from hearing good things about our selves and about the other family members we live with.

A BACKGROUND OF GOOD IDEAS

Some families play Self-Talk on cassettes in the background while they are getting ready in the morning, over breakfast, or when they are going about their daily activities at home.

When Self-Talk is practiced in the home, it is not unusual, for instance, for even a young child, four or five years old, to notice when someone else makes a *negative* self-talk statement of the old kind.

One mother told me a story about her young son, Kevin, who had overheard the Self-Talk cassettes she and her husband had been listening to each morning for about two weeks. Kevin had frequently heard his parents discussing the Self-Talk they were using, but they had not yet told him what this new "Self-Talk" was or why they were practicing it. One morning, as she was rushing out the door for work, Kevin's mother said, "I have a feeling it's going to be one of those days!" "What is one of those days?" Kevin asked. His mother answered, "A *bad* day." The profound response from her five-year-old stopped her in her tracks: "If you say that, it will be."

It is a healthy sign when a young girl or boy recognizes a negative self-direction when she or he hears one. It lets us know that the youngster has gotten the message, is becoming aware of his or her *own* self-directions and is aware of replacing the wrong words with something better.

PRACTICING SELF-TALK AT HOME

I have received many excellent suggestions from people who have practiced a variety of ways of putting Self-Talk methods to work in their homes.

Some of these ideas may not apply to you or members of your family. But some that have worked for others should work for you, too. They are some of the best ideas I have found for helping create family relationships that work, and they are an exceptionally good way to create togetherness and unity within a family.

1. Set aside an evening each week to spend one hour with all of the family members to discuss their goals and how their Self-Talk can affect them.

2. Sit down privately with each family member and talk about his or her current problems—and what Self-Talk they should be using to help deal with the problems.

3. Spend some time each week listening to Self-Talk as a group—either from a cassette tape or from individual Self-Talk cards that family members write for themselves.

4. Discuss old programs and write out new Self-Talk to replace them.

5. Give a small award for the best Self-Talk written by a family member. Make sure that everyone—especially the children—gets some prize for making the effort.

6. Set some family goals, and write Self-Talk phrases that all the family members can use to reach those goals.

7. Play a game called "What Should You Say?," which asks each family member, in turn, how to change a negative statement into a positive Self-Talk statement.

8. Set aside one day each week in which no one is allowed to say anything negative. Anyone who slips up has to do extra chores.

9. Mom and Dad, or Mom or Dad, if there is only one parent at home, spends one day each week saying only good things about each of the children. (No suggestion was received about what to do if there were more than seven children.)

10. If there are just two of you—husband, wife, or special person—then for one week each month each person should write out a list of the other person's ten best qualities and read them out loud to that person.

11. Give a special prize to the family member who can complete the phrase "I like myself because . . ." using the best reason. Once again, any good answer should get a prize.

12. On the family bulletin boards, put up cards which state whose board it is, with the additional words "I am . . .," and thumbtack cards under the name that give positive descriptions about that person, such as, "I am . . . always on time, smart, a happy person, tidy, getting better at math," and so on.

Those suggestions should give you an idea or two. Right now, there are husbands, wives, parents, grandparents, friends, and new acquaintances who are creating their own forms of how to learn Self-Talk, or are teaching Self-Talk to somebody else.

Their methods may be different, but their goal is the same: to help themselves or make someone else feel better about who he or she really is. As we learn about *self*-direction, it is almost automatic that we want others to feel better about themselves.

When a family uses Self-Talk in the home, as a normal part of everyday life, it is that kind of awareness among *all* the family members that begins to affect and change how they talk to each other. It changes how they respond to disagreements or problems; it affects how they relate to each other in almost any situation.

Parents, of course, are usually the first to recognize the potential effects of what they say to their children. Once you realize that anything you say to someone else—especially children—is programming that person in a way that could affect his or her entire future, you tend to change very quickly some of the old programs you have been giving them.

When you understand the results that are created by

your own Self-Talk, you begin to recognize that there is a wrong way and a *right* way to talk to anyone about anything. Knowing that can create immediate as well as long-term benefits in the home.

CREATING A SELF-TALK ENVIRONMENT IN THE HOME

When Self-Talk is talked about and practiced in a family, the Self-Talk itself goes to work to begin creating positive results for the individual who uses it. But it also creates a different *environment* in the home. I have seen homes where people somehow survived within a daily environment of turmoil—constant squabbles and disagreements, emotional overreactions, and other old-style everyday behaviors that are guaranteed to create stress and tension.

With better Self-Talk, some of those same home environments change. The family members are now more agreeable, more willing to listen and work things out, and adopt a more positive approach to everyday problems and situations.

However, practicing Self-Talk at home—even when all of the family members are enthusiastically involved—does not suddenly turn family life into a utopian, problem-free environment. Life still throws a lot of surprises and problems our way, and we have to deal with them. But it is *how* we deal with all of those daily situations in the home that Self-Talk affects.

When, as family members, we begin to look at each day in the same new way, with new Self-Talk, we set up a home environment that encourages working together to make things better. We don't ignore the problems. We don't hide our heads and pretend that the problems don't exist. When we, and everyone else around us in our own home, begin to take responsibility for creating solutions, then *home* becomes a better place to live.

When you are working at making a better home, Self-Talk isn't the only answer. But because Self-Talk brings out the best in you—and encourages the best in others—it helps you create a way of thinking, a way of doing things, a way of relating to others that makes being together something better for everyone. It gives you a better chance of achieving what you created your home for in the first place.

Imagine giving your loved ones the gifts of self-esteem, self-belief, and personal responsibility. Can you imagine what those gifts could do for a young child who someday will have to face having to say yes or no—stand on his or her own two feet—or give in to the pressures of the crowd?

Imagine giving something to someone you love deeply that will help that person feel better about himself or herself, make better decisions, see you and others in a more accepting and understanding way, and take responsibility for making decisions that could affect your life *together* in the most positive way possible.

The more I have learned about Self-Talk, the more I have come to believe that it is the best gift we can ever give to our selves. The more I see Self-Talk go to work in families and homes, the more I believe it is the most important gift we can ever give to the people we care about most.

THE STORY OF THE WORDS

In Part II of this book I have compiled some of the best and most effective words of Self-Talk. Whether you read them, or listen to them on tape, or use them in some other way, remember that the words of Self-Talk are only the flint that strikes the fire. Use the words of Self-Talk to set your self up. Use them to challenge you to change—if you want to change; to do better—if you choose to do better.

No one else is going to write your story for you. No one else is responsible for writing the story of who you are, who you will become, or what you will do for the rest of your life.

We are a human race of living words. We live by words. They create many of our emotions, tell us where we are, and give us most of what we know about our selves. All too often we have thought that words were nothing more than parts of sentences written in books, or spoken by us—parts of thoughts, arranged in groups, and defined by the characters of an alphabet that give sense and structure to our thoughts.

But every word you and I will ever hear, think, write, or speak will have a picture and a meaning attached to it which

123

inform and stimulate the programming files of our sub-conscious minds. We are affected by our words—*each and every one of them*. Our words carry the life-giving breath of awareness that courses through our minds; they are the es-sence of our understanding and our motion through life. Our Self-Talk tells us who we are, how we feel, and what we should do about every moment of our existence.

IT ISN'T THE WORDS THEMSELVES— IT'S THE NEW PICTURE THE WORDS CREATE

We have learned that in spite of the profound importance of the words we use when we talk to our selves, it is not the words themselves that are important, it is the awareness and the *habit patterns* which the words create in our minds that matter. But without the words themselves, most of us have no place to start.

Long ago I saw the fallacy of relying on just the Self-Talk itself. It isn't the Self-Talk we teach our selves that counts—it is our awareness of it, and the long-term program changes which the Self-Talk encourages, that make the difference; what matters is the pictures the words create in our con-scious and subconscious minds—through repetitive use. For this reason, starting with the right words is one of the most important things we can do.

The words we have used to talk to our selves in the past may have been used by chance. The words we use to talk to our selves tomorrow need not be. Those of us who learn the difference have a choice. Once we recognize that the choice is ours, we realize that our own lives are *not* the result of chance; they are the result of our own thoughts, the clear, simple directions we give our selves.

I once received a letter from a man who had learned to believe the wrong things about his life, and used the wrong words of programming about himself. He wrote to me from a prison cell, where he is living out the rest of his life, paying his debt to society. In his letter he told me that he had just recently learned about Self-Talk. He had finally learned, through Self-Talk, that it was not *life* that put him there; it was his own internal picture of himself. Once we realize how the mind works—why we do what we do—it doesn't make any sense for any of us to become prisoners of our own programming.

THE WORDS OF SELF-BELIEF

I have said that there is no mystery, and no magic, in Self-Talk. Self-Talk is, after all, a rather simple procedure, a "first small step" to something else. But it *is* a step, and it is important. If you were to glance at the section of this book which contains the phrases of Self-Talk without understanding their meaning and use, I suppose those words could be seen as only a collection of inspirational verses, positive in content and appropriate for times when you need the right motivation to pep you up or get you started. But the words of Self-Talk go far beyond the inspiration and motivation they offer.

Just as we have been told that our eyes are the mirrors of our souls, so are our words the mirrors of the messages we give to our minds. We have come to recognize that *we are what we think*. We have also come to realize that *what we think* is almost entirely governed by the words we use.

The story of *your* words will ultimately become the story of you. What you say to your self about you will affect, and to a large extent control, what happens to you all through your life. If you are looking for a boost along the way, the words of Self-Talk in this book should help you get started.

The picture you have been painting of your self in the past is becoming the picture of who you are today. The words *you* decide to use now will paint the picture of your future. Given a little time, your own words today will become the story of you, tomorrow.

C·H·A·P·T·E·R
SEVENTEEN

THE SELF-TALK
SOLUTION

Is the Self-Talk Solution, then, a final solution? Is the Self-Management which Self-Talk builds, a practical new answer for what ails us? There are many who say that it is. The concept of Self-Talk is now being studied and proved by medical researchers, educators, therapists, and leaders in the field of human behavior, who claim that Self-Talk is one of the most effective tools they have found for implementing worthwhile and lasting changes in our individual lives. The evidence in favor of the beneficial effects of Self-Talk and Self-Management is too strong to discount or ignore.

Self-Talk breakthroughs and individual success stories are now daily occurrences. The uses of Self-Talk are reaching into every segment of our society at every level of behavior.

The reason for the overwhelming acceptance of Self-Talk as a significant new tool with a broad variety of uses is that *it works*. The results are clear: Self-Talk is one of the most fundamental solutions for dealing with human behavior that we have ever found. And there is no chance or luck involved; *there are good reasons why it works*.

126

The principles of Self-Talk and Self-Management are being used so widely because they are principles which are *natural* to our own minds. So many of the solutions that we had thought we had found in the past proved not to be solutions at all. Too many of them depended on an individual's background or education, or life-style, attitudes, or beliefs.

The use of Self-Talk is completely indifferent to any of our past beliefs or misconceptions about our selves. The concept of Self-Talk treats us all the same. The effects of our own self-directions are not the result of some so-called success system; they are an end result of a normal activity of the human brain.

In the past, when we wanted to make some change in our selves, whether to become more in control of our selves, change a particular habit, or set and reach a new goal, we were at the mercy of a biochemical-electrical computer that was designed to follow rules which, in the past, we were not taught. The understanding of that fact is proving to be one of today's most important discoveries.

Some years ago, when I first began to explore the theories about the relationship between human behavior and the chemistry of the mind, I suspected that we were on the right track. Since then, those theories have been tested and proved countless times.

The effect of self-direction on the human system is no longer a theory; it has proved to be a sound medical and psychological truth. The relationship between what we think and how well we do throughout our lives—and, perhaps more important, how well we do each day—has moved from metaphysical speculation to scientific certainty. The physiological process of Self-Management is not a theory, it is a fact of life.

REAL PEOPLE WITH REAL RESULTS

One of the many schoolteachers who have been teaching Self-Talk to her students, and playing Self-Talk tapes in class each morning, wrote me about some of the remarkable changes that her students had made after practicing Self-Talk over several months. Because the teacher was researching the use of Self-Talk as a regular classroom-curriculum program for her school district, she sent me a detailed outline of the progress each of her pupils was making.

Along with the stories of slower students getting better grades, of an entire classroom having fewer "bad" days, of students getting along better at home, and of students with low self-esteem seeing themselves now as bright and positive, I found that one of her pupils, in particular, had an especially inspiring experience.

Throughout most of the school year, Michael, an eighth-grader, had problems. He was tough, difficult, usually in trouble, and failing in his studies. His dress, attitude, behavior, and indifference to classwork were all working against him. For several months he had not shown up sober at a school dance or activity. Because of his low self-esteem, Michael had become the perfect example of a problem teenager.

The Self-Talk tapes his teacher played for the class, once each morning and once in the afternoon, gave the students basic statements about self-esteem, personal responsibility, getting things done, studying and concentration, and setting and reaching personal goals—all standard, frequently used Self-Talk tapes. Each Monday the teacher selected a new Self-Talk subject, discussed it with the class, and then used that Self-Talk tape for the entire week.

Almost unnoticeably at first, Michael's attitude began to change. He started to get to class on time and his attendance became more regular. For the first time he began to show an interest in class, and his marks began to move slowly from "fail" to "pass." He began to spend more time talking to the other kids in his class, and began to make friendships with other students he would only have fought with at the beginning of the school year.

By the end of the year, Michael had surprised his teacher, his parents, his friends, and most of his classmates. But it was when he showed up at the end-of-the-year school dance that he surprised everyone the most. He arrived well dressed and with a haircut, and he was sober.

What impressed me most about Michael's story is what he told his classmates. "I don't need that other stuff," he said. "I didn't used to like myself. Now I do."

In a different sort of story, Karen, the mother of two, had

quit her job as an account executive for an advertising agency to raise a family. When Karen left her job, she was attractive, in touch with her career, very capable, and making a good income. After twelve years away from the outside world, Karen decided to go back to work. Her "problem" was that, in the meantime, she had convinced herself that she was unattractive, overweight, and underqualified to get and hold a job.

When I met Karen at a seminar I was conducting, she appeared to have a natural ability to brighten up any room she walked into. But during the seminar, she admitted that it was her own self-doubts that had held her back from achieving any of the new career goals she had set for herself. "I have gotten four job interviews in three weeks," she told me. "One of them, the first one, I went to, two of them I canceled, and the fourth one is next Monday. I came here today to find a way to get enough self-confidence to go."

Since I strongly believe that self-confidence has to come from within, I told Karen that she might have come to the wrong seminar. "All I can do," I said, "is show you what you can do for your self." But Karen stayed, listened, and went home and began to work on her Self-Talk.

Several months later, I received a greeting card from Karen. It read as though it was written by a different person than the Karen I had met at my seminar. She told me that she had jumped headfirst into using the new Self-Talk for the "new Karen." She had lost sixteen pounds of what she called "the unnecessary weight of unnecessary self-talk," found a job with an advertising agency, and had received her first bonus a month ahead of schedule. On the front of the card she wrote: "I'm back!"

Karen proved a point. Her own self-direction, her own sense of self-esteem had struggled with a picture of her self that had not been true at all. The real, "inside" Karen, the attractive, capable professional, just needed the right Self-Talk—from Karen to her self—to bring back the professional Karen.

I once received a letter at Christmas that I doubt I will ever forget. It was from a thirty-nine-year-old man who, just eighteen months earlier, had decided that his life was no longer worth living.

In his letter Thomas told me that on a Sunday evening, when he had finally decided that he no longer wanted to live, he looked for bullets to load his gun to end it all. He wrote: "After thirty-nine years of struggle I had decided it wasn't worth the effort to go on living. I was broke, I had sabotaged all my friendships, and lost the business that I had worked at for thirteen years. It seemed to me that nothing was working, and I had no idea why."

As Thomas sat on his couch, holding a gun and contemplating his future, which, as he wrote, "was to end in a few minutes," he overheard a television program about Self-Talk, which was playing on one of the cable networks in his area. It was a program in which I talked about replacing our old programming by using self-direction—and, as a result, giving ourselves the chance to create a new future. His letter went on: "I began to hear this voice on the television telling me why I was where I was, and that I could redirect my life to get the results I desired. What I heard was enough to momentarily stop me."

By the end of his sincere, and sometimes painful, letter, Thomas told me the story of his road back, how he sat down that night and began to write out new Self-Talk for himself, how he recorded his own Self-Talk and listened to it over and over. "The first days were rough," he wrote, "but what I was hearing began to make sense."

The new self-directions Thomas gave to himself took root and grew. Today Thomas is not only among the living, he is busy with a new career and inspiring others to live *their* lives to the fullest.

The teenage boy who learned, from listening to Self-Talk tapes in school, that his own self-esteem could replace alcohol or drugs and bad behavior, did not make the changes within himself because of luck or a freak accident of his own nature.

The woman who lost her professional self-confidence and got it back twelve years later, did it on her own by changing the words she was saying to her self.

The man who decided to end his life, and then resurrected himself from self-doubt by changing his *self*-direction, gave himself a new future.

Each of these people was willing to try the simple idea of replacing old programming with something better.

These are *ordinary* people who, through a minor change in their self-directions, experienced extraordinary changes in their lives. The thousands of other real-life individuals who have used Self-Talk and Self-Management to lose weight, change habits, improve their marriages, increase their sales, organize their lives, or make surprisingly positive improvements in their attitudes have not done so because of a chance encounter with some new-style self-help technique. *They made the changes simply because they used one of the oldest and most natural physiological principles of the human mind.*

AN ALMOST INSIGNIFICANT STEP TO A SIGNIFICANT NEW WAY TO LIVE

The simple concept of Self-Talk, and its goal of Self-Management, have had a profound effect on the people who have learned it and put it to work for themselves. Imagine what our own Self-Talk could do for us if we did nothing more than adopt it and use it as many others are now doing. If what we have learned about the behavior of the brain has created a trend that continues to grow, many of us fortunate enough to be alive today could be among the first to witness the quiet, powerful beginnings of change in an unusual number of people.

We are fortunate to be living in this age. The idea of managing our selves is taking hold; it is an idea whose time has come. The concept of Self-Management is one of those truths that strike an inner chord in each of us.

If we do nothing more than follow the directions and stay on the course we set for our selves, in less than a generation or two, we could find that Self-Talk, and its accompanying methods of Self-Management, have become a natural and accepted part of our lives. We might find that a simple form of Self-Talk is taught and practiced in even more schools, in books for children, in our jobs, with our families and friends, and as a natural part of the environment of our homes.

For just a moment, imagine living a life among people who had learned to direct the incredible resources of their own minds. Imagine living a life in which fear, self-doubt, insecurity, uncontrolled emotions, and old, self-limiting programs did not *rule*. Imagine a generation of children brought up with the knowledge and the tools that would one day give them the solid armament of self-direction, self-esteem, and the pride of personal responsibility.

There is no telling what even one generation of self-motivated, *self*-managing individuals could do. What strides they could make! To those of us who have watched Self-Management work its subtle wonders in people's lives, there is no doubt that they could accomplish more than we could ever have hoped to achieve in our own lives. We have spent too much precious time struggling through the accidental, misdirected programs of our past.

There is no telling what we could do if we instead spent our time living out lives which were created by each of us having a hand in the conscious self-directions of our own futures.

GO BACK TO THE TREASURE— AND OPEN IT UP

I began this book by telling you about finding a treasure chest—whatever it may have contained. It is not only a story that happened in my own life; in another way it is a true story for most of us.

There is, perhaps, no Shangri-La for anyone. There may be, in the realities of everyday living, no perfect solution. I doubt that, at least on earth, there ever will be. But I have come to believe that having the courage to find and uncover the best of our selves is far better than leaving our better selves buried somewhere in our past disbeliefs. We may never find perfection—we should not even try—but if we do not take the time to look for what *is* there, there is a good chance that we will *never* find the best of our selves.

There is a treasure chest within each of us which many of us could have found and opened—but never did. For most people, the treasure is still there, waiting to be discovered. *Until our last breath is taken, it is never too late to go back, find the treasure chest, open it up, and live it out.*

Somewhere, buried deep in the words of your own Self-

Talk, *if you look,* you will find parts of your self that have been waiting for you for a long time.

The right *words,* contained in the right kind of Self-Talk, are just examples of the words that are the very best descriptions of *you.* Not all of these words will lead you to the treasures of your self, but some of them will. Some of them will tell you the *real* truths about who you are and what you would *really* like to do with your life. They are like a photo album, filled with the snapshots of the real you—mental pictures of the treasure you hold within your self.

If you would like to find this treasure, read the Self-Talk self-directions in Part II of this book. When you find the words that speak to you, about *you,* make them your own. Change them, add to them, give them the energy of your own conviction. Use them to create for your self a little more of the treasure that is *you*—that you have wanted to uncover all along.

No one else can find you *for* you. Bringing out the best in our selves is something that no one has ever been able to do *for* us. If we really want to find the treasure, and live it out, we will have to do it for our selves.

The treasure is you. It was all along. But it is up to you to find it, scrape the old soil of the past from the top of the chest, find the lock, open it, and put to use the best of what you find inside. If you do that, you could find the "solution" you have been looking for.

I can offer you some of the most effective Self-Talk I know of for getting you started in the right direction. But from this moment on, it is up to you to recognize what the solution *really* is, and what it could mean to you *in every thought you have for the rest of your life*. The Self-Talk Solution is real. It is reliable. It is a part of you that has been there all along—and it works. The Self-Talk Solution is *you.*

P·A·R·T

II

THE WORDS OF
SELF-TALK

The words you will find in this section are starting points. They are stepping-stones to creating, if you stay with it, an awareness of your own past self-talk and of the kinds of self-directions that work. They are not meant to be the ones you will use in every case, after practicing your own Self-Talk, but they are a practical way to get started.

Compiled in this section is, to my knowledge, the most comprehensive collection of Self-Talk phrases that has been put into print. Without any doubt, there is something here for everyone.

Find the words that talk to you about *you*, and put them to use. They will show you, by example, the kinds of words and phrasings that work best when you are starting to create your own Self-Talk.

I would also recommend that you use the words in another way. I will never forget the time several years ago when I was studying Self-Talk, and had placed a small stack of individual Self-Talk cards on the nightstand beside my bed. On them was some of the same Self-Talk which appears in this book. Almost by accident one evening, just before I turned out the light, I decided to take a few minutes and read through those cards.

As I read each of the cards I experienced something which I can only describe as exhilarating. When I read those simple words and phrases to my self, one after another, an exciting new conviction was created within me.

I did not know then that what I was feeling was more than an emotional response to the words; it was a natural physiological (chemical) response to solid, self-directed thoughts.

I was *inspired!* I felt *good* about my self! I felt encouraged, uplifted, and a great deal more self-confident than I had felt just moments earlier. Could a few written words do that? I was to learn later that a few simple words—of the right kind—could not only make us feel better at the time, they could also have a profound effect on our health, our attitudes, and a host of other areas of our lives.

After you have read the words and found those that speak to you about your objectives, instead of putting the book away on the shelf, reopen it frequently to Part II, The Words of Self-Talk, and reread a page or two. The words may catch you as they caught me. They may give you a glimpse of your self that will make your day brighter and better. When a problem arises, or when a goal is strong, read the words again. They will focus your thoughts, direct your objectives, and *pre*play the result which you would like to attain.

Remember that the words are a tool to help you learn the first step toward making it an *internal,* unconscious, natural habit to use Self-Talk. Your old self-talk was a way of life for you in the past; there is no reason why your new Self-Talk should not become a way of life in the future.

If someone had told me that I could write only one book, and in it I had to write the best of what I had learned about the *self* that lives within each of us, I would have written *The Words* of Self-Talk. It is the *words* that we give to our selves that will always determine how we think. It is the words that we give to our selves that will always determine how we *live*.

These are the words I would like to give to you. In time, I hope that they are the kinds of words which, without even thinking about it, you will give to your *self*.

EIGHTEEN

GETTING STARTED WITH SELF-TALK

This chapter contains the kind of Self-Talk that will help you start creating a stronger overall picture of your self—it is a Self-Talk that works with the *attitudes* you have about your self. Too often we want to make a change without first getting a fix on the attitudes that created the problem in the first place.

This Self-Talk script gives you self-directions about believing in your self, setting goals and working at accomplishing them, taking responsibility for your self, and creating the determination to go after what you want and stay with it. And it talks to you about your self-esteem, how to bring out more of the *person* in your *person*ality.

In the script that follows, you will find much of the person you *already* are, and more of the person you might like to become.

When you read these Self-Talk phrases, find those that apply to you and use them as often as you can. The more you think about who you would like to become, the more possible it will be.

BELIEVING IN INCREDIBLE YOU!

This Self-Talk script, like many of those that follow, is nearly universal in approach: Its words apply to anyone, at any time. It is also one of the Self-Talk scripts that many people find especially motivating, the kind of self-direction that helps you get started in the morning, or gives you an extra boost of enthusiasm. It is a Self-Talk that tells you, "If it can be done—*I can do it!*" If I had to select those scripts that *always* seem to help make each day a little better, this would be one of them.

I know that greatness begins in the minds of the great. I know that what I believe about my self is what I will become—so I believe in the best for my self!

I am practical and realistic, and I keep my feet on solid ground. But I also give my self the freedom to live up to my fullest expectations.

I never limit my self by the shortsighted beliefs of others. Instead I open my self up to the broad horizons of unlimited possibility.

When someone says "I cannot," I answer, "Why not?" When someone says, "It's impossible," I answer that nothing is any more impossible than I believe it to be. And with my individual fortress of faith, with me, anything is possible.

I have drive, spirit, stamina, and endurance. I have a good strong winning attitude about my self and about everything I do. I am practical and realistic, but I also believe in the best possible outcome of any situation.

If I have ever had any doubts about my self in the past, today is a good day to put them aside. It's a good day to throw out any disbelief that ever held me back.

I know that I am headed in the right winning direction, and I look forward and never look back. I have the ability to focus on one thing at a time, so I concentrate my attention on the job at hand—and I get it done!

Today is one of those days when nothing can stand in my way. When I need extra determination, I've got it! When I need more energy and drive, I've got it! I've got the power to get it done and the patience to see it through, no matter what the job or challenge may be.

Right now, even while I am telling my self these truths about me, I know that I can succeed and I am succeeding. At this moment, if I think of any challenge in front of me, I know that I will become even more a winner because of it.

I keep my chin up, my head held high. I look, act, sound, think, and feel like the winner I am! Anytime a problem starts to get me down, I get my self right back up! I tackle problems and I solve them. When frustration or defeat threatens me, I just become that much stronger, more positive, better organized, and more determined than ever!

Right now, today, this very moment, I am capable of giving my self the gift of absolute self-assurance, self-belief, and powerful nonstop confidence in my self.

No matter what it is that requires the very best of me, I can do it and I know I can.

Today is a great day. And I've got what it takes. So I choose to do it right, do it well! I choose to live today with joy and love.

I know it's all up to me. One hundred percent! Every bit of it! All of it is in how I look at it and what I do about it! That's what winning is. That's why I am a winner.

I set my sights. I keep my balance. I don't hesitate. I don't hold back! I know that the world is full of opportunities. Look at what I can do; look at where I can go! Look at what I can do just by saying "Yes" to myself!

Just look at what I can do today! I am incredible . . . and today is a great day to show it!

SETTING AND REACHING GOALS

It is unfortunate that most of us were not taught the powerful results that setting simple, realistic, specific goals can create. Basic goal-setting skills are easy enough to be taught to schoolchildren, and they can last a lifetime.

There are good practical reasons for setting good practical goals. One of them is that goals focus your attention and help you define some of the things you'd like to accomplish. But another equally important reason for setting goals is the effect that *accomplishing them* has on your self-esteem.

If you achieve something, let's say, an increase in income, an improvement in being more organized, or an award for winning a sales contest, it may make you feel good about your self. But if you accomplish an objective after you have written it out as a clearly defined *goal,* you can give your self a gold star for doing something that *you specifically set out to do.* That gold star goes right on your list of personal accomplishments that build more self-esteem. You are able to say, "I wanted to do it; I made the decision to do it; I made it part of my plan; *and I did it!*"

The following Self-Talk creates an awareness of goals—and sets up your subconscious mind to make goal setting a natural part of your everyday self-directions.

I set goals. I write them down, and I review them often.

My goals give me a clear picture of my own positive future—in advance!

I spend several minutes each day reviewing the goal cards I write for my self. I read my goals to my self each morning when I awake, and each night just before I go to sleep.

My goals are very specific. The more detailed and specific they are, the more clearly I am able to visualize them and create them in my life.

Every time I see something in my self that I choose to change, or decide on something that I want in my life, I write it down, set a goal, review it daily, act on it, and achieve it.

My goals are my road map to my own future. I plan where I am going, how I will get there, when I will arrive.

I am successful when I achieve my goals, but I am also successful each day of the journey. I know that success lies not only at the end of the road, but in each step along the way.

I set daily goals, weekly and monthly goals, and goals that set my sights a year or more in front of me.

By setting short-, medium-, and long-range goals, I stay in touch with where I am today, and I give positive, active direction to where I will be tomorrow.

I take absolute responsibility for who I am and where I'm going. By setting goals, and working daily to achieve them, I take responsibility for determining my own destiny.

I choose to live my life by choice, not by chance. Setting goals and working to reach them keeps me in control of my life.

I consciously make the decisions that affect my life and my future in the most positive possible way.

Anytime I want to make a change or achieve anything in my life, I write it down, along with my plan to accomplish the goal and when I will achieve it. In this way I turn each of my goals into action.

By writing out my goals, I am actually writing my own script for the story of my future. By following my specific action plan, I turn my dreams into reality.

If, along with your Self-Talk for setting and reaching goals, you would like to create a simple Goal Plan, get some five- by seven-inch index cards and write one specific goal on the top of each card. Below that, write the numbers 1, 2, 3, and so forth; these are the *specific* steps you will take to reach that goal. After each step, write down when you accomplish that step.

Then, in order to get into the habit of working with your

goals, read through each of your goal cards every morning or at night just before you go to sleep. Because it works best to set only a few goals at a time—no more than three or four to start—reading through them a time or two should only take a few minutes.

I recommend listening to the above Self-Talk for setting goals *while* you are reading through your goal cards and thinking about each of them. Do that for thirty days as a start and watch what happens. You will keep your self on track, accomplish more, and give a boost to your self-esteem and peace of mind.

TAKING RESPONSIBILITY FOR YOUR SELF

Learning to take *personal* responsibility for every one of your thoughts and actions is one of the prime ingredients in all personal growth. Many people have made the words below their number-one Self-Talk script to use along with any other script they are working on at the time. It is the kind of self-direction that puts you in charge of *you.*

The old self-talk that helps us avoid responsibility may not sound harmful by itself, but listen to the programming it gives us: *"That's not up to me"; "It's not my responsibility"; "I just can't decide"; "That's just my luck"; "It's not my fault"; "It's just not fair"; "I don't have any say"; "Don't ask me, I just work here"; "They're always pulling something";* or *"I never get a break."*

This is exactly the kind of self-talk that takes away your responsibility for your self. There is a better way to talk to your self.

I take full responsibility for everything about me—even the thoughts that I think.

I am in control of the vast resources of my own mind. By using my own new winning self-directions, I direct and control what I say when I talk to my self. I alone am responsible for who I am, what I do, and what I tell my self about me. No one can share this responsibility with me.

I also allow others to accept their responsibilities for themselves, and I do not try to accept their responsibilities for them.

I enjoy being responsible. It puts me in charge of being me—and that's a challenge I enjoy. I allow no one else, at any time, to assume control or responsibility over my life or over anything that I do.

My responsibility to others is an extension of my own winning responsibility to my self.

I choose to leave nothing about me up to chance. When it comes to me—and anything in my life—I choose to *choose*.

My choices are mine alone to make for my self. I do not, at any time, allow anyone else to make my choices for me. I accept full responsibility for every choice and decision I make.

I always meet all the obligations which I accept. I accept no obligations I will not meet.

I am trustworthy. I can be counted on. This is because I have accepted winning responsibility for my self—and I always live up to the responsibilities I accept.

There is no "They" on whom I "lay the blame," or with whom I share my responsibilities. I have learned the great secret of mastering my own destiny. I have learned that They—is *me!*

I joyously accept that I am not a victim of the circumstances of my life. I create the winning life I live. I am the author of my own script.

In my life I am the winner. I am not the victim—I am the *victor!*

I have no need to make excuses, and no one needs to carry my responsibility for me. I gladly carry my own weight—and I carry it well.

Each day I acknowledge and accept the responsibility not only for my actions—but also for my emotions, my thoughts, and even my beliefs.

I accept the responsibility for my strengths, for my happiness, for my positive, healthy attitudes—and for my past, my present, and my future.

I have received letters from people who told me that they used that script of Self-Talk over and over before using any other Self-Talk scripts, because personal responsibility was the one area they really felt needed fixing. The interesting comment that many people have made, however, is that just by using that single script, they began to make improvements in *other* areas of their lives that had little to do with responsibility—at least directly.

Without knowing it, they were proving a point that is worth remembering. When you take responsibility for your self, you take responsibility for everything else about you.

LEARNING TO SAY NO

If you want to say yes to success, you have to also say no to those things that get in the way of your self.

Learning to say no is more than simply deciding *not* to do something; learning to say no is *learning to trust your own judgment*. When you practice making choices for your self, you automatically build up your self-confidence. In time, setting your own course becomes easier and more natural. The old habits, the past programs that got you to give in and get by, give way to new habits of thinking and acting for your self. It doesn't mean you will refuse to listen to good ideas; it will mean that the final choice will be up to you.

These are the self-directions that get you thinking about making the right choices.

I like being the person that I am. I like the way I think. I believe in my self, and I respect my decisions and the choices I make.

I respect my self. I respect my values, my thoughts, my ideas, and my actions. And I respect my self most when I follow the path which I set for my self.

I always say no when no is the answer I should give.

Not giving in to the demands or the influence of others makes me even more aware of the freedom and self-control that I have in my life.

My time is important to me. I carefully guard the time which I set aside for the things which are important to me. I allow no one to take my personal, special time away from me.

I am always able to help others most when my own needs are met. Taking care of my self at all times is a responsibility which I accept and always live up to.

I invest my time and my energies where I choose. My time and my energies are gifts which I guard and give by my choice— but never by the demands, dictates, or the expectations of others.

I live my life by choice, not chance.

I never give in to the persuasion or the demands of others . . . unless I choose to agree for reasons of my own.

I allow no one to "sell" me on anything that I do not genuinely choose to accept. I live my entire life by my own decisions— never by the pressures or the selling skills of others.

I never, at any time, feel any obligation to do anything that I do not honestly choose to do. I say what I think. I am forthright, direct, and honest. I know what I want and where I stand, and I express my opinion clearly and without hesitation.

Saying no is easy for me. I am confident, self-assured, and in control of my life.

People respect me for being myself and for standing up for the things I believe. The stronger I am, and the more I live by the decisions which I choose for my self, the happier I am.

DETERMINATION AND WILLPOWER

Many successful people will tell you that one of the most important habits they learned was the habit of refusing to give up, even when the going got tough.

Whether you want to lose weight, stand up for yourself, study harder, reach a professional goal, get along better with someone close to you, lower your stress and relax more, or achieve any other practical goal, the determination to achieve your objective may be the deciding factor in your success.

What good can it possibly do to program your self with *"I just don't think I can"; "I'm ready to give up"; "What's the use!"; "This is too tough for me"; "I'm not up to it"; "I'm tired of trying"*; or *"I know this won't work"*?

Since nothing worthwhile is ever gained for free, it's possible that the obstacles of having "dues to pay" along the way may try to get you to give up, or put off your goal. Obstacles may be a way of life but, with practice, so is determination.

I know that in any success plan, determination is the ultimate ingredient—and I have determination.

I am totally committed to the achievement of the objectives which I set for my self—not 50 percent or 99 percent, but 100 percent committed to the full realization of my goals.

I am a winner. I make decisions about my self. I set my own goals. I determine my own course and direction. And I allow no one else to make these decisions for me.

An accurate description of me would include the words: strong-willed, decisive, steadfast, persistent, and determined.

I am a winner. I am absolutely determined to achieve my aims. I am steadfast and persistent in the pursuit of my goals, and I will not give up.

I am able to see a precise picture of exactly what my goals are in everything I do—and what I must do to achieve each of them. I have my plan clearly written out, and I follow it every day.

Each time I decide on a specific goal—of any kind—and a specific plan of action to achieve that goal, I fix my sights firmly on my objective and set out doggedly to achieve it.

What others call "defeat" or "failure" does not stand in my way. I know that what most call "failures" are nothing more than detours along the way. So I move past them and keep on going.

No defeat is ever the end of the road for me. I know that roads don't stop—people do. So I make sure that my roads keep going and so do I. I keep moving and that keeps me winning.

Because winning takes energy, good health, and a strong, positive attitude, I make sure that I keep my self fit—both mentally and physically.

I have a healthy attitude about my self. I genuinely like my self. I have a positive self-image and a lot of respect for who I am.

Because I accept my self and like who I am, I know that I really deserve the right to win in my life.

And that gives me the determination to win—more every day, and in the most positive and worthwhile way.

I have courage. I meet my challenges with the confidence of knowing that I have the stamina to endure and the determination to succeed.

I have strong convictions about winning—and strong convictions about keeping my self in "winning condition."

Each day I recognize my absolute determination to reach all of the goals that I set for my self in every area of my life—at my work and in my personal life.

I am able to actually see my self achieving my goals. And every day I become more positive and more determined than ever!

BUILDING SELF-ESTEEM

The natural result of all the Self-Talk in this book is stronger self-esteem. But the following script focuses on self-esteem itself. It is one of those Self-Talk scripts that you could use every day for the rest of your life—and you would still not be using it too much.

I really am very special. I like who I am and I feel good about my self.

Although I always work to improve my self and I get better every day, I like who I am today. And tomorrow, when I'm even better, I'll like my self THEN, too.

It's true that there really is no one else like me in the entire world. There never was another me before, and there will never be another me again.

I am unique—from the top of my head to the bottom of my feet. In some ways, I may look and act and sound like some others—but I am not them. I am me.

I wanted to be somebody—and now I know I am. I would rather be me than anyone else in the world.

I like how I feel, and I like how I think, and I like how I do things. I approve of me and I approve of who I am.

I have many beautiful qualities about me. I have talents and skills and abilities. I have talents that I don't even know about yet. And I am discovering new talents inside my self all the time.

I am positive. I am confident. I radiate good things. If you look closely, you can even see a glow around me.

I am full of life. I like life and I'm glad to be alive. I am a very special person, living at a very special time.

I am intelligent. My mind is quick and alert and clever and

fun. I think good thoughts, and my mind makes things work right for me.

I have a lot of energy and enthusiasm and vitality.

I am exciting, and I am really enjoying being me. I like to be around other people, and other people like to be around me. People like to hear what I have to say and know what I have to think.

I smile a lot. I am happy on the inside and I am happy on the outside.

I appreciate all the blessings I have, and the things that I learn, and all the things I'll be learning today and tomorrow and forever—just as long as I am.

I am warm, and sincere, and honest, and genuine! I am all of these things and more. And all these things are me! I like who I am and I'm glad to be me.

DEVELOPING A WINNING *PERSONALITY*

Your personality is the "you" that you present to the rest of the world. It is the picture that you give to everyone around you (and to your self).

Your "personality" is not something you were born with, and it is not something you are stuck with. Most people who have noticeably good personalities have had to create them. How you feel about your self even for a single day can have an effect on how you feel, act, and get along with others that day.

No matter how good or strong your personality is now, you might like to practice showing the world your *best* personality for even one or two days. I have seen people get surprising (and positive) reactions from their family members, friends, and work associates, just because they took the effort to work at their personalities for a day or two. One or two days of effort won't actually change your programming, of course. But it will show you what you *could* do with your self if you wanted to.

If you'd like to see that better personality continue, keep changing the old programming and replace it with the better picture of your self. Tell your self, *"This is the way I choose to be. This is the me I would rather give to my self and to the other people in my life. From today on, this is how I am!"*

The success of many of the opportunities that come your way, each day and throughout your life, will be affected by the personality you present. The personality you present will *always* be the one you create in your own mind.

I have a winning personality. I am friendly, enthusiastic, warm, and real. I am the kind of person people like to be around.

People like me. They like many things about me. And one of the things they like about me most—is the way I am with them.

I am genuine and sincere with everyone. I treat everyone I meet with courtesy, respect, deference, and consideration.

I am attractive in many ways. I attract others to me. I attract their interest, I attract their enthusiasm, I attract their friendship, and I attract their faith. I attract the very best in everyone—and, therefore, I am attractive.

I have respect for others, and they have respect for me. I regard everyone I meet as being important to me. I create a feeling of trust and respect quickly and easily with people.

I have a sunny disposition. I practice having a bright, warm, worthwhile outlook on life.

I am sincerely interested in others, and it shows. People are important to me, and I let them know it.

I am a good listener. I listen to others with a genuine concern for their beliefs, their thoughts, and their ideas.

I always allow others to express themselves completely and freely. I am attentive and encouraging anytime anyone talks to me.

I look for the "quality" in everyone that I meet, and I always find it.

I am always considerate of the feelings of others. I am aware of their feelings, sensitive to their attitudes, and mindful of their beliefs.

One of the reasons people like to be around me is that I always make people feel good about themselves.

I always show those around me the very best of who they are.

Each day my own personality becomes brighter and stronger, and it shows even more clearly the positive, winning spirit within me.

NINETEEN

SELF-TALK FOR FAMILY AND RELATIONSHIPS

In this chapter you will find Self-Talk for creating belief and worth in marriage, becoming a better listener, dealing with intimacy in a positive and fulfilling way, and improving relationships.

In an earlier chapter we talked about using Self-Talk at home. Getting into the Self-Talk habit—and helping others in the family to do the same—can create noticeable results. How you feel about your self and others can—and often does—determine whether your home life is happy or not. Whatever the quality of your home life at present, the Self-Talk that follows could make a positive difference.

SUCCESSFUL MARRIAGE

There are few other aspects of life that are affected as directly by attitudes, beliefs, and feelings as a strong, enduring relationship with another person.

It is also true that marriage can create some of our greatest challenges, while at the same time giving us some of our greatest rewards. A marriage can create, almost in the same moment, a blending of oneness and difference; and it places on both partners an obligation to do their utmost to make the blend work.

If marriages are, as they say, "made in heaven," it seems that "heaven" has left it up to us to learn how to be a better "partner" (which means to be "a part of" another person).

The following words of Self-Talk may not suddenly turn problems into solutions or frustrations into bliss. But they are self-directions which, if you make them *your* words, will help you build and nurture the spirit of your relationship. No good marriage is a casual event left to chance. A good day-in, day-out relationship is the result of love, patience, dedication, honesty, understanding, caring, belief, effort, and support.

These words do not describe lives that work only for "someone else." They are a few self-directions that you, and the person you love, can put into practice for your selves.

I enjoy being married and experiencing the many benefits and blessings which marriage brings to my life.

My marriage works—because I work at it. I do not take success in marriage for granted, and I recognize the role I play in keeping my marriage working and growing.

My marriage is proof that teamwork pays. In my life I am never alone. I am always part of a caring, loving, winning team.

I believe in the power of setting goals and in working for the goals we set and achieve together.

I genuinely admire my partner, and it shows. I express my admiration and approval often—both in public and at home.

I respect my partner's uniqueness as an individual. I admire the many special qualities which this brings to our relationship.

I care about who I am, and in my marriage I take responsibility to be my self.

I am loving, considerate, thoughtful, and caring—both for my partner and for my self.

I keep my self in great shape, mentally and physically—both for my partner and for myself.

I like the way I look and feel, and I like keeping my self that way.

I like the way my partner looks at me, and I know that it is a reflection of my own approval and appreciation in return.

Any disagreement we have is always dealt with in a private, understanding, and considerate way.

I respect my marriage and my partner, and I always work to resolve any disagreements in the most positive possible way.

I am honest, sincere, and open in my thoughts and opinions. I express myself clearly and with consideration for my views and for the views of my partner.

I am proud of the way I communicate with my partner, express my thoughts and feelings, and hear and understand each thought and feeling being expressed to me.

I do not see marriage as a place to control or be controlled by. I rely on the love, support, and belief of my partner, but I alone am in control of my self and my life.

The more responsibility I take for my self, the more successful my marriage becomes.

Imagine practicing that kind of Self-Talk by yourself, or with your partner, each day or even now and then. I have known couples who, on the occasion of a wedding anniversary, repeated their marriage vows to each other as a way of reaffirming their commitment. Imagine keeping the hopes and dreams of your marriage alive—not just on your anniversary, or on some special day, but every day of the year!

In your own relationship, you and your partner might

like to try a technique that can yield far-reaching results: One evening a month, read the above words of Self-Talk out loud to each other. During the rest of the month, say them to yourself now and then, or even every day. It will take only minutes. But living out the results could last a lifetime.

POSITIVE PARENTING

It's a good idea to understand how you feel about your responsibilities—especially responsibilities as important as raising children. The Self-Talk in this script creates a picture of a healthy attitude about parenting. It is the kind of self-direction that lets you see your role of parent as a positive "guide" for your child.

We have all heard, and some of us have used, self-talk for parenting of quite a *different* kind. Look at just a few examples of what some people tell themselves about one of the most important responsibilities—and *blessings*—they will ever have: *"I don't think I was ever cut out to be a parent"; "My kids will be the death of me"; "I just can't talk to him (or her) anymore"; "I just don't have the time"; "Sometimes I can't stand my kids"; "My youngest is nothing but trouble"; "They really get under my skin"; "What did I do to deserve them?"; "My house is always a mess"; "Teenagers are impossible!"; "Nothing I do seems to work"; or "Where did I go wrong?"*

The Self-Talk below is different. It lets you know that being a good parent is one of the most valuable gifts you can give to someone else—and to your life. It creates an internal attitude that is nurturing and loving, but it also encourages you to allow your children to begin to see their own "very best pictures" of themselves.

I am an exceptionally good parent! I like being a parent and it shows in every part of my life.

I accept the responsibilities that parenting brings to my life. I am up to them, I meet them, and I welcome them.

I am good at helping children learn to see themselves in the most positive possible way.

I create harmony and happiness in my home.

I am a good listener. I always listen with interest, understanding, and love. I let children know that I can be talked to—and that I listen!

I am strong and determined, but I am also understanding and supportive.

I never parent with idle threats or forgotten warnings. I can always be counted on to be true to my word.

I understand the difference between punishment, discipline, and training, and I always work to keep them in their proper perspective.

I can be counted on. Because I am reliable and consistent I greatly increase the assurance of love and security in my home.

I teach values by the examples I set.

I see each day as an opportunity to show, by example, the very best way to live that day.

I never criticize or belittle a child's efforts or ideas.

Instead of expecting "perfection," I expect the best that my child has to offer.

I am good at giving rewards, big or small, and at any time at all.

I make it a point to tell each member of my family something special and good about that person each and every day.

I keep my self up, enthusiastic, and in good, healthy spirits.

My own positive attitude about parenting is reflected in everything that I do.

I really enjoy being a good parent and experiencing the many joys and benefits that positive parenting brings to my life, and to the lives of those I love.

BECOMING A BETTER LISTENER

How much more we would hear if only we listened. *Not* listening causes misunderstandings, misinformation, and countless problems. *Listening,* on the other hand—active, vital, *aware* listening—can help you open your mind to a whole new realm of possibilities for being in touch with your life.

I have never yet met an aware, successful, self-controlled man or woman who was not also a good listener. Developing the skill of listening also develops the skills of concentration, awareness, perspective, visualization, and communication. I have known people who seemingly *never* listen. I have known others who always talk—instead of listening—only because their own insecurities about themselves forced them to do so.

Of the five senses with which the human brain gathers information, seeing and hearing are foremost. Most of us have the equipment we need; any of us can learn to use it better. But the Self-Talk in this section talks to you about the kind of listening that goes even beyond the physical capability of hearing. It conditions you to "listen"—to perceive, pay attention, and focus your thoughts on the moment at hand.

Whether you are in school, making a sales presentation to a customer, talking to a child or a spouse, or listening to a friend, you can, at any time you choose, turn the dial of your mental receiver, tune in, concentrate, and hear more of what is really being said.

This Self-Talk script on learning how to be a good, positive listener has started to work almost immediately for anyone who has tried it. Try it yourself. Read this script three times before your next meeting, before you go to work tomorrow morning, or just before you plan to have an important conversation with someone. The long-term results could create some noticeable benefits for you. Even the *short*-term results may surprise you.

I am a good listener. I am always gracious, polite, attentive, and positive. My interest in others is bright, alive, and enthusiastic—and it shows!

When someone speaks to me, I always "listen up," I never "listen down." I am always openly and positively attentive no matter who is speaking to me or what he or she is saying.

I am an especially good listener at home and with the people I love most. I always listen to understand. And my understanding and the caring that it shows add greatly to the warmth and happiness of my friends and family.

I never spend time planning my next words when I should be listening to what is being said now.

I hear everything the speaker is saying—not just part of it. I never look at listening as waiting my turn to speak. When I listen—I listen.

When someone is speaking to me, I let him know that I am giving him my full attention. My face shows my interest and always shows the attention I am giving him and the words he is saying.

When someone speaks to me, I listen for agreement and commonness of thought. I listen for oneness of purpose and unity in our goals.

Listening positively shows in my face and in my voice.

People are naturally more cooperative and friendly when they speak to me.

I always let people know that I am listening to them. I make it a point to feed their thoughts back to them when it is appropriate, to share my understanding of them.

I am a careful listener. I do not listen just to hear. I always listen to understand.

I also listen when no words are being spoken. And it is often then that I hear the most.

I listen not only to the thoughts of others, but to the voice that speaks from within my self as well. I listen to this inner voice carefully. This is the voice of my best friend and counselor, and I heed the advice which it gives me.

Each day I become more and more skilled in the language of positive listening. I enjoy practicing and improving my listening skills every chance I get—and I practice them with anyone I talk to, or listen to, anywhere I am.

IMPROVING PERSONAL RELATIONSHIPS

This Self-Talk gives you a picture of how important others are—and how you see your self dealing with them. How you relate to people has a lot to do with how they relate to *you.* How you see your self will always affect or determine how *other* people see *you.*

When you deal with another person, you automatically, and usually unconsciously, go through a "process" in dealing with that person. The process starts with how you feel about your self. That mainly determines how you feel about someone else. That, in turn, affects how you act toward that person. And that affects how the *other* person will act toward *you.* And, of course, the way people treat you will almost always determine how you treat them back!

To get the best results from others, it makes sense to get started on the right foot—liking who *you* are and expecting the best from your relationships with the people around you.

People are important to me. I feel good about the people in my life, and I know they feel good about me, too.

I automatically attract others to me who are honest and sincere, and who value my beliefs as I value theirs.

My personal relationships are warm, meaningful, and richly rewarding. I am genuine and sincere at all times and with all people I meet—regardless of the situation or their relationship to me.

Although I do not demand a doctrine of fairness from the world around me, I am always fair in my dealings with others.

I believe in people. I greet each new relationship with faith and acceptance, and I consciously build the relationship toward trust and respect.

I am able to express my feelings toward others, and I am patient and understanding in their expressions toward me.

I listen when people speak to me. But I listen to much more than the words they say; I listen most to the messages that come from within.

I find something that is good in everyone I meet. I look for and find a quality of value in each person. I have a high regard for others.

My friendliness is genuine and my sincerity is real. Because I like, enjoy, and accept others, friendliness and sincerity are habits with me.

I am always ready to give the benefit of the doubt in any situation. And when in doubt, I always assume the best possible thing.

I make friends easily, and I have great respect for the friendships I make. I can be counted on. People can rely on me in any relationship.

I am trustworthy and responsible, and people place great value on these qualities in me.

I would rather give than demand, and I choose to accept rather than judge.

Every day I am even more consciously aware of my relationships with others, how important they are, and the great value they hold in my life.

CREATING INTIMACY

Each of us has the right to create and experience fulfillment in our lives. Intimacy and sexual fulfillment are most certainly two of the most wonderful blessings that God ever bestowed on mankind. If they weren't, I doubt that He would also have given us a psychological makeup and a chemical hormone system that placed so much importance on that part of our lives!

If there are any limits imposed on the expression of your self—physically, intimately, and in other ways—it should help to know that those limits are almost always imposed by your past programming. *What you have come to believe, fear, or accept in the past has nothing to do with what you yourself are capable of achieving in the future.*

The Self-Talk in this script is designed as a starting point for recognizing your own natural need and right to fulfill and be fulfilled. You may want to add words of your own that specifically address you. Let your self know that you deserve to experience and fulfill every part of you. Your sexuality is one of the finest, most essential, and most worthwhile facets of who you are.

I feel good about my self. And I experience fulfillment in all areas of my life.

I am aware of my self. I believe in my ability to express my self physically, spiritually, and emotionally—without reservation and without holding back.

Expressing my self intimately and sexually is one of the greatest joys of my life. I give my self the freedom to experience joy—completely and fully.

I am warm, sincere, loving, considerate, and caring. These are qualities which I possess, and I find them also in others.

I love to touch, and I do. I am able to easily and comfortably express my self physically with the individual of my choosing.

I am a GREAT partner! I know how to relax and create fulfillment for BOTH of us—just by being me!

I enjoy giving, but I also enjoy receiving. I deserve to receive an abundance of joy and pleasure in my life, and I give my self the absolute and irrevocable permission to enjoy!

I am in touch with my most intimate feelings and desires. There is a rich, warm treasure of beautiful intimacy within me.

I know that expressing my self sexually is good. It is a positive and important part of my total well-being.

I take the time to let my partner know my needs and to share in the creation and achievement of my fulfillment.

I give my fantasies the freedom to live in my mind and to add to the beauty and joy of my relationship.

I like the body I have created for my self. It is part of who I am, and I like being me.

I experience complete fulfillment. My intimate personal experiences are deeply satisfying and richly rewarding.

I view my self and my own intimacy with enthusiasm and with positive expectation. I believe in the best for my self. I am worthy of the best and the best is what I get.

I value my self, and I recognize that I am capable of living to my fullest potential in every area of my being.

I like who I am, and I live my life every day in the freedom of my own self-acceptance self-belief, and in the joy of expressing my self completely and fully.

I live life at my best, physically, spiritually, and in every other important area of my being.

I release my anxieties about my self, and I let them go.

TWENTY

SELF-TALK FOR FITNESS AND HEALTH

Some of the Self-Talk that I am asked to write most often is the kind that helps us get into better shape physically. It is important Self-Talk because changing even the subtlest physical habits, not to mention helping us achieve such major goals as stopping smoking or losing weight, *has to* start with how we *see* our selves *inside*.

It is because some of our attempts at making physical changes have proved to be losing battles in the past, that we become convinced we will never win. As a result, and because the goal is not only psychological, it is also physical, and often genetic, making any lasting changes requires the best mental programs we can create.

Self-Talk, by itself, will not work miracles; it was never intended to. But it could be the tool that makes the difference. If you are presently using some method or technique to lose weight, stop smoking, reduce stress, or reach some other physical goal, by all means, if it is working, stay with it. But every day add a healthy dose of the mental nourishment that Self-Talk gives you.

I know of no other area of personal change in which the *repetition* of Self-Talk is more important. It is when we are confronted by our own *physical* constraints and habits that we need every ounce of encouragement we can get.

Find Self-Talk that is right for you, or write your own; but by all means *use* it. Use it over and over, use it every day, use it when some obstacle seems to slow you down or stop you. Use the Self-Talk when old temptations strike or when you start to lose sight of the goal.

There is a reason why we use the expression "Practice makes perfect." It is because so much of what we do is the result of the *strongest* patterns we have set up in our own minds. And that, as we have learned, is the basis of Self-Talk. That is why practicing Self-Talk, over and over, con-scientiously and actively, plays such an important role in helping you change a habit or reach a goal. If you want to change the old habit, the old physical *pattern,* you have to change the mental pattern first.

Even with Self-Talk, the job may not always be easy. But used often enough and strongly enough, your own Self-Talk will always make a difference.

OVERALL HEALTH AND PHYSICAL FITNESS

The following Self-Talk script, and the other scripts that tie mental attitude to physical health, are becoming some of the most widely used. This is not surprising. The relationship between physical health and mental attitude is becoming one of the most popular areas of present-day research.

Today, many medical practitioners are beginning to teach their patients that a healthy mind is the foundation for a healthy body. I suspect that within not too many years, one of the chief medical preventatives of disease will be the mind itself.

Meanwhile, from Olympic competition to professional athletic teams to personal-fitness programs, a growing body of evidence suggests that how you think (even *while* you exercise) will affect your results.

There is a clear relationship between your health and physical fitness—and how you program your self. The following Self-Talk will give you an idea—and a basic format to follow—that will pair your best mental skills with your best physical potential. It is a short course of *"health food for the mind."*

I feel great! My mind is sharp and clear. I am physically fit and healthy. My energy level is high. My attitude is excellent. And I am organized and in control.

I am aware of my own physical body and its importance to my total well-being. I always do what I need to do to keep my self in excellent shape and condition.

My body is the storehouse of my mind. It is important to me to keep both my body and my mind well tuned and working for me.

Good health comes naturally to me—but I never take good health for granted. I am healthy, I feel good, and I am proud of the amount of positive attention I give to keeping my self that way.

I eat and drink only those things which are beneficial to my physical and mental health and well-being. I never eat or drink more than I should, or do anything that is harmful to me in any way.

Because I take good care of my self at all times, I have an abundance of physical drive and stamina. My endurance is excellent, and I am full of life and energy.

My lungs are clean and strong. I am able to breathe deeply and fully.

I exercise each day—and I enjoy it! I look forward to the feeling of exhilaration and well-being which exercise gives me.

I listen to the voice within me, which always tells me the truth about my own physical fitness and condition. I never ignore its warnings, and I always heed its advice.

I weigh exactly what I should. Because I maintain a healthy balance of diet and exercise, maintaining my proper weight is easy for me.

I always give my self the right amount of rest and relaxation. I get all the deep, restful, replenishing sleep that I need.

Each morning I make sure that I wake up completely rested, fully refreshed, and in great spirits!

When I look at my self honestly in the mirror, I like what I see. I am proud of my self for the great job I'm doing of keeping my self looking and feeling this good!

My mind takes good care of me. I consciously condition my mind with my own self-directions, to keep my body fit, healthy, and filled with strength and energy. My mind does this for me at all times and without fail.

REDUCING STRESS

Few subjects in the field of self-improvement during the past few years have created as much interest as the effects of—and the reduction of—stress in our daily lives. Most of us have come to recognize the effects that the wrong kind of stress creates within us, both physically and psychologically.

Doctors are continually advising their patients to slow down, take some time off, relax, take up a hobby, or change jobs. I received a call from a woman one day during a radio talk show in Cleveland, Ohio. The woman, who was named Elaine, told me that she knew she could solve most of her problems if she could just have some time to herself. She worked full time, had two young children, had recently re-married, and was trying to make everything work at once. She was giving all her attention to others, but she could not find any time for herself. In her words, she was "frazzled, at her wits' end, and ready to quit."

I asked Elaine, "How can you do your best for everyone else when you don't take the time to do your best for your self?" I told her a story about a high-school coach who had been in an automobile accident, but because he refused to take the time to get better, he was trying to teach the track team how to run and jump hurdles while he was still on crutches.

You can't do your best for anyone else in your life when you haven't taken care of your self. That may sound selfish, but it is just the opposite. Unless you learn to relax, give your self some peace of mind, and recharge your own batteries, how can you possibly think, respond, act, or do your best at *anything?* Take the time to get rid of your own stress first, and you will find that you get a lot less stress coming back at you from the world around you.

Of all of the stress-reducing methods we know of, one of the best is learning how to stop stress where it starts: in the mind.

Many of the Self-Talk scripts you will find in this book will help you reduce the causes of stress in your life. When you set goals, take action, overcome problems, get your self in shape physically, and accept the responsibility for your own role in life, you begin to resolve, in a natural way, many stress-creating problems.

Daily use of the Self-Talk in this script, however, has helped a lot of people overcome the *effects* of stress, and offered them a way to slow down, clear their minds, and practice making stress-free relaxation a normal part of their day.

If you would like to develop more quiet self-confidence, recharge your energies, and enjoy the benefits of feeling good about your self, these are some of the words that will, if you use them each evening (or any time you want to relax), help you control stress and its effects.

I am calm and confident. I have the quiet self-assurance of winning in my life.

Relaxation is important to me—and I always get the right amount. I make sure that I take not only the time to work at achievement, but also the time to enjoy the beauty of life along the way.

I choose not to spend my life trying to live up to the expectations of others. I allow no one to impose the pressures of their

demands on me without my choice, my acceptance, and my approval.

I consciously and unconsciously remove all harmful stress from my life. I allow only those energies which are positive and good for my total well-being to work within me.

I view my life and everything in it from the calm, clear perspective of great awareness and understanding.

I have inner peace. I am living my life in a positive and worthwhile way. I have purpose and value. I like who I am and I enjoy being me. And this creates even greater peace and self-assurance within me.

I give fear no place to dwell in my life. I am much too busy living a life of positive fulfillment to allow any time or space for fear, or the stressful consequences it creates in others.

I prevent, in advance, harmful stress from occurring in my life. I meet my responsibilities enthusiastically, I confront conflicts and I resolve them, I never overcommit, and I get things done on time.

I always keep my long-range goals in front of me.

I am very aware of those surroundings which have the most positive, calming, and relaxing effect on me. And I create those surroundings for my self in many areas of my life.

I never allow harmful tension to build up inside me. I conquer stress by conquering its causes. I consciously remove stress and its tensions through long-range perspective, simple goals, appropriate action, and good, healthy exercise.

I am in control of my emotions. I never get needlessly upset or overreact to any situation at any time.

I often practice "feeling" relaxed in my mind. When I want to relax completely, even for a moment, I go to the place in my imagination where I find an immediate and never-failing sense of inner peace.

I feel the quiet peace of complete relaxation and contentment within me. Each time I repeat these words in my mind, I find my self becoming even more self-assured, relaxed, and free from stress in all things and in all areas of my life.

SELF-TALK FOR EXERCISING

No one needs self-motivation more than the person who wants to exercise, starts an exercise program, and wants to stay with it. When you are working to improve your self *physically,* you need all the motivation you can get!

But if you are like most people, you don't have a personal coach to keep you up and going, pushing you, *demanding* that you push your self, never letting you give up or put it off—unless, of course, you learn to create that "coach" for your self.

But listen to how some people "coach" themselves about exercising: *"I get started but I just can't stay with it"; "I would love to exercise more if I had the time"; "I just don't have the energy I used to"; "I'm not as young as I used to be"; "I really need to get started"; "I know I should"; "I put it off"; "I'm so out of shape"; "I just can't do it"; "Exercising is really hard work"; "I ache all over"; "This is tough"!; "I don't know why I put myself through it";* or *"I don't know if I can take another day of this."*

Exercising may demand a lot of you. But with *that* kind of programming, it is no wonder that exercising is "tough!"

There is a better way. It will not make the aches and pains go away, but it will make you feel a lot better about getting your self in shape. And the Self-Talk in this script will do one other thing: *It will help you stay with it.* As I have said before, your *best* coach is *you.*

Use this Self-Talk the next time you exercise. If you use a cassette, play the tape *while* you are exercising. I have learned to *enjoy* exercising by playing this Self-Talk on a small cassette player while some lively, up-tempo music plays in the background.

I know many successful—and healthy—people who listen to this Self-Talk wearing personal headphones while jogging, running, riding a bicycle, or doing exercises at home in their living room. It gives them the immediate, on-the-spot motivation of an "outside coach," while at the same time, it creates more permanent, long-term programming that affects how they feel about themselves physically *and* mentally.

Try it. If you would like to be at your best *physically,* and feel *good* about it at the same time, here is some Self-Talk that should help you get the job done.

I really like being in good shape! I take care of my self and I keep my self fit.

I enjoy exercising. When I exercise I can feel my self getting stronger, healthier, and in top condition!

I set fitness goals for my self and I follow them. I follow a regular plan of exercising, good nutrition, and the right amount of rest. I keep my self in shape in every way.

When I set a goal, I reach it. I stay with it, and nothing can stop me!

I really like the positive effects that exercising creates in my life. And that gives me even more motivation to exercise every day!

When I know I should go on but think that I can't, I give my self the powerful words of encouragement which say, "You can do it, keep at it, don't stop! Reach your goal! You deserve to reach it and you will!"

I like my self. And I like the fact that I take the time to take care of my self.

I'm a great coach! I keep my self up, motivated, enthusiastic, and going for it!

Exercising is good for me. It helps me keep in the best shape and in good health. Exercising keeps me alert, feeling good, and living at my best!

I look good already, but I look better every day. I am proud of how I look, how I feel, how I think, and how I live!

I enjoy the "high" of being healthy—the exhilaration I feel when I'm exercising. The feeling that exercise gives me is worth every ounce of work I put into it.

I like the challenge of getting in shape and staying in shape. I am up to the challenge and nothing is going to stand in the way of my success.

I create a picture of my self, the way I want to be, in my mind. I set my goal, I see it clearly, I work at it, and I reach it!

I do everything I need to do to keep my self healthy, very fit, and feeling good.

I always get the exercise I need, and I don't quit until I reach my goal—every day and anytime I exercise.

I never overdo it, or harm myself physically or in any other way. I get exactly the right amount of good, healthy exercise.

I have learned to enjoy exercising, but I also visualize in my mind the benefits that my exercising is creating for me in the rest of my life. I look good, I feel great, and it shows in everything I do!

I enjoy exercising now more than ever before. I have incredible determination and a nonstop attitude. I exercise and I like it!

Every time I exercise I feel even better about my self. I am really proud of my self for the great job I'm doing!

If you have ever struggled to overcome the "stoppers" that try to get in the way when you want to get into top best physical shape, *that* is the kind of Self-Talk you should use. It reminds you to stay healthy, it forcefully demands that you do what you set out to do, it motivates you, and it shows you the benefits that *you* create by doing it. What a difference this Self-Talk can make.

Enjoy the Self-Talk, but, more important, *enjoy* your exercise!

SELF-TALK TO STOP SMOKING

Most of us would agree that there is every good reason not to smoke. For those who never smoke it is usually common sense and reason that keep them from starting. But once you start, and the habit is created, it takes more than just "reason" to stop.

When someone continues to smoke, it's the result of several factors that in the past worked together to make smoking a tough habit to break. The best way to defeat the habit is to "divide and conquer." The principal factors that promote and affect this habit are:

1. Mental image—your self-concept as a smoker

2. Psychological dependency—repetitive pattern of behavior

3. Physiological dependency—chemical addiction to nicotine

Many people who stop smoking for a time, and then start again, often do so because they have overcome *one* of the factors, or even two of them, but have failed to recognize and deal with *all three*. Some smokers talk of having stopped for months or even years and then starting again—long after the chemical addiction was gone. The actual *physical* dependency on nicotine usually lasts only for a few weeks after you have stopped smoking. That means that your need to smoke is no longer physical, it is psychological—it is a habitually patterned behavior, a self-*image* in which you continue to see your self as a smoker.

SEEING YOUR SELF AS A HEALTHY NONSMOKER

Your ability to change a habit ultimately depends on how you see your self and what you believe most about your self—consciously and unconsciously. If you continue to see your self as a smoker, chances are you will continue to act out that belief. If you begin to see your self as a *non*smoker, your subconscious mind will direct you to live the role of a nonsmoker.

If you are a smoker, some of your past self-talk may have sounded like some of the statements below that smokers often use:

> *I've tried but I just can't seem to quit.*
>
> *When I stop smoking I gain weight.*
>
> *I smoke to relax.*
>
> *When I'm around other smokers I've got to have a cigarette.*
>
> *I enjoy smoking.*

Turn these statements around.

Along with good nutrition and plenty of exercise, and using any other effective method for quitting, your new Self-Talk can help you quit. It will also help you leave the old habit behind as you create a *new* habit of visualizing your self as a *non*smoker.

I do not smoke.

My lungs are strong and healthy. I am able to breathe deeply and fully.

Taking care of my self physically is important to me. I keep my self fit and feeling good.

I am a nonsmoker—and I am proud of my self.

I have more energy and stamina than ever before. I enjoy life and I'm glad to be here.

When I see a cigarette, or even think of one, I automatically hear the words "I do not smoke"—and I don't!

I have no habits which control or influence me in any harmful way. I am in control of my self and every thing I do. I always do what is best for me, my self, and my future.

I really enjoy breathing clean, fresh air, being healthy, and being in complete control of my body and mind.

I am able to achieve any goal which I set for my self. I see, in my mind, a clear picture of my self having already accomplished my goal. I create it, I see it often, and I achieve it!

I exercise regularly. I keep my self fit and healthy. And I am enjoying a lifetime of energy and vitality.

All of my senses are clear and alive. My sight, my sense of smell, my hearing, my sense of taste, and even my touch are more alive than ever before.

I do not see smoking as being strong, intelligent, or glamorous in any way. I see it for what it really is, and it has no place in my life.

I give my self permission to relax, feel good, breathe deeply and fully, and enjoy being a healthy nonsmoker at all times and in all circumstances.

People enjoy being around me. I have self-confidence and self-respect. I like my self, and it shows!

Being a nonsmoker is easy for me. After all, I was born that way—and it is the natural way for me to be.

I am a *non*smoker! *I do not smoke.*

ENERGY AND ENTHUSIASM

We sometimes recognize that we would feel better and get a lot more done if only we had more energy and enthusiasm. But having extra energy and enthusiasm is up to us.

You can create more physical and mental energy by learning to create enthusiasm in your mind. When you create a strong enough *reason* to be more energetic—a new energy *program*—the extra energy will not be far behind.

I feel great today! I have more energy and vitality than ever.

I am able to accomplish many great things. And with each accomplishment, even more energy comes to me!

I have a high energy level—and my interest and enthusiasm keep it that way.

My level of energy grows stronger and more dynamic each day. I am full of life, fit in every way, and in exceptionally good spirits!

I have the capacity to achieve every objective I set for my self. Every goal that I set is always matched with the energy and enthusiasm that I need for its accomplishment.

The more I concentrate on my objectives and visualize their attainment, the more enthusiasm I develop and the more energy is created within me.

Challenges are stimulating and invigorating. I meet each challenge I face with determination and drive, and with an absolute assurance of the most positive possible outcome.

I am awake, aware, and ready! I have plenty of pep and ambition. I meet every opportunity with drive and enthusiasm.

I keep my self in excellent physical condition. I give my self more energy by exercising regularly each day.

When I am doing something which requires extra energy, I am always able to summon a reserve supply, and I always have more than I need to get the job done.

I get the rest I need—both for my body and for my mind. But I never rely on rest alone to build my energy for me.

I build my enthusiasm by keeping my interest level high! The more interested I become in anything that I do, the more enthusiasm I have. The more enthusiasm I have, the more energy I create.

I always picture in my mind the positive outcome of anything that I do. Pictures of my goals, which I see clearly in my mind, create within me an energy chain which is powerful and unfailing.

I regularly program my mind with positive instructions to keep myself fit, energetic, and filled with youthful enthusiasm.

My awareness of my own energy and vitality is growing daily. I am creating an unlimited abundance of energy within me.

GETTING TO SLEEP

Not being able to get to sleep easily, or stay asleep once you nod off, can have a variety of different causes. In some cases the problem is physical—and should be treated medically. But in many cases a sleep problem is the result of something troubling the mind.

We have all known times when we cannot sleep because of a problem with a relationship, or because things are not going well at work, or because of nearly *any* kind of worry at all. I have known people who solved their insomnia by finishing a task that they had been putting off. Once they got the job done, the insomnia went away. Other people have cured sleeplessness with an improvement in their diet; others have found the answer in a regular program of healthy exercise.

Because not being able to sleep is so often tied to some other "problems" we are facing, the following Self-Talk was written to deal with those problems, as much as it was written to deal with sleep itself.

I should point out that this script is *not* "hypnosis"—it is Self-Talk, in one of its most relaxing and quieting forms. But I recommend that you read this script to your self or listen to a Self-Talk cassette only when you are ready to sleep. It is Self-Talk that lets you see your self and your life in a calm, confident, healthy, and self-assuring way.

I have been surprised by the number of people who, over the years, have asked me for a complete script of Self-Talk for insomnia. Most of them asked if I would record a tape that they could listen to when they wanted to "come down," tune out, relax, and go to sleep.

So I recorded one of my most unusual Self-Talk cassettes. It doesn't really "inspire"; it quietly convinces and persuades. It is a tape of your most gentle self, tucking you in, and telling you, "Good night." After I was finally convinced to record that cassette, I ended up listening to it myself when sleep had trouble coming to me.

If getting to sleep has been a problem for you, here is some of the Self-Talk from that tape.

It is time for me to sleep. It's my time to rest.

I'm ready to relax. Today has been great, but now I need to sleep.

I have peace of mind. I am confident, relaxed, and at peace with my self and with my life.

I enjoy the quiet, restful peace that I create in my mind.

My view of life gives me a perspective of balance—and I see things as they *really* are—in their proper place of importance in my life.

I have learned to relax. I now relax my self by giving my self permission to put to rest any thought that could have created tension or worry in my mind.

I relax my self physically and mentally. I let my self float in the secure feeling of peace and absolute contentment.

When I want to go to sleep, I visualize a quiet place of perfect peace in my mind. I see it, I feel it, and I rest in the complete security that it gives me.

Just before I go to sleep, I tighten and relax each set of muscles in my body, beginning with my feet, and moving upward throughout my body. I remove, from each muscle, all tension and stress.

I am calm, relaxed, and ready to sleep.

My life is good. I deserve to rest and to sleep, free of worries and free of cares, and filled with the quiet, relaxing assurance of an even better day tomorrow.

I am at peace with my self. And I find my self thinking only those thoughts which give me even more tranquillity and peaceful relaxation.

I feel very content. I like the peace which I feel in my mind and in my body.

I am happy with my self. My life is orderly and in control. I am able to go to sleep easily and naturally, and I sleep well.

I am relaxed. Life is good. Life is working well.

Sleep makes me feel good. It comes to me and puts everything out of my mind.

I consciously remove all unnecessary thoughts from my mind and I let them quietly drift away. If they are important to me, I will think about them another time. But for now, I let my thoughts rest.

I'm going to sleep now.

Good night, my friend. Sleep well.

SELF-TALK FOR WEIGHT LOSS

Because I receive many requests for Self-Talk for losing weight, controlling snacking, changing eating habits, and keeping the weight off, I have included here an extended collection of Self-Talk on those subjects.

One of the areas of Self-Talk that has generated much public interest is using Self-Talk for losing weight. My own television programs on the subject of Self-Talk for weight control have generated literally thousands of letters and phone calls from people who wanted to learn more about it.

Weight control also happens to be one of the areas in

which the *results* of Self-Talk are the most obvious; these results can be measured by looking in the mirror or by standing on a bathroom scale. But in spite of the many successes people are having in making conscious changes in their self-directions in order to lose weight and keep it off, results will come only if you practice, practice, and then practice some more.

I produced a complete series of eight different Self-Talk cassettes on weight loss and weight maintenance. I have included a few of the Self-Talk phrases from several of these cassettes here. This is one of the many areas of Self-Talk that I have had good reason to use for my self in the past. I, too, was pleased—"excited" might be a more accurate word—to see that this Self-Talk helped me solve a weight problem I had spent several years creating.

I have now seen the effects that this same Self-Talk has had on countless others who have used it. I am confident that used in the right way and given time and determination to succeed, it will do the same for you.

I look great and I feel great! Looking and feeling good is one of the many rewards I receive for keeping my self fit and trim—and I keep my self that way!

I take responsibility for my self. I alone determine how I look, how much I weigh, and how I feel.

I eat only those foods which are beneficial to me.

I never eat more than I should. I know the amount of food that is right for me, and I am proud of my self for eating right, thinking right, and looking better than ever!

I enjoy eating less. Although I always get the nutrition I need, I really enjoy having small portions and a small appetite.

When I sit down to eat, at any meal, I say to my self, "I live best when I eat less."

I eat only those foods which benefit me and keep my weight where I want it to be.

I choose to be healthy, energetic, and attractive. I make sure I fit the clothes I like. I think about this every day, and every day I get fit!

I know that how I look, what I weigh, and how I feel are entirely up to me, and I do everything I need to do, each day and each moment, to create the me I really choose to be.

GETTING STARTED WITH WEIGHT LOSS

I have made the decision to take control of my self—and that includes how I look and what I weigh.

I know that the best way to get started is to begin by believing in my self, taking control of my life, and seeing my self the way I really want to be.

I know that my weight depends entirely on how I see my self, and what I say when I talk to my self. I have learned to see my self becoming slim, trim, healthy, and very happy.

I begin each day by concentrating and focusing on becoming my new self. I set my goals, I review them each day, I see my self achieving each of them, and I reach them!

Getting started is easy for me now. I do everything I need to do to reach and maintain the weight I want.

I am ready and willing to pay the price to look and feel the healthy way I want to. After all—I'm worth it!

I like my self better already. Changing my self is changing my life—in many positive and worthwhile ways.

The more I listen to my new self, the more I recognize the me that has been there all along.

CONTROLLING BETWEEN-MEAL SNACKS

I have willpower, self-belief, and self-control. I am in control of what I eat and when I eat—and that includes during meals and in between!

When it is right to have a snack, I choose food that is light, nutritious, and healthy.

I no longer snack out of habit or replace proper meals with unnecessary snacks. I now eat regular meals, the right food, and just the right, healthy amount.

I never snack to relieve anxiety, nervousness, tension, or loneliness. I resolve my problems by recognizing them and by working on them—never by replacing solutions with snacks.

I no longer snack to pass the time, or for something to do while I'm reading, working, talking, relaxing, or watching TV.

Each day I successfully control between-meal snacks. I have created the healthy new habit of winning at weight loss. I am a winner—and I prove it—every day!

SITTING DOWN TO EAT

Whether eating out or eating in, I really enjoy eating less.

I never feel the need to finish the food in front of me. I eat only what I should—and never one bite more.

One way to weight loss that's easy and works is less food on my plate, and less on my fork.

By ordering less when I eat out and by serving my self smaller portions at home, I keep my self aware of the importance of staying with my goal.

When I sit down to eat, at no time do I allow anyone else to influence, tempt, or discourage me in any negative way. I have learned to say no to the food, and yes to my success.

KEEPING IT OFF

I have lost the weight I wanted to lose—and I make sure I keep it off.

Maintaining my weight is easy for me now. I have learned to eat right, exercise more, and keep my mind and my body fit and healthy.

My mind automatically keeps me at the weight I want to be. My mind does this for me easily, at all times, and without fail.

I have created the habit of thinking, acting, and living in a healthier new way! I no longer feel the need to eat more than I should, or to do anything that would work against me or keep me from the freedom I have achieved by reaching my goal.

I think, act, feel, and live differently now. Right now and at all times, I see my self in a whole new trim, attractive way.

When I am faced with any situation which in the past would have added needless weight, I now immediately say to my self, "I don't need it—and I choose not to eat it. I took it off and I'm keeping it off!"

Every day, instead of gaining weight, I now gain self-esteem!

There is other Self-Talk too, not necessarily written just for weight loss, that will also help. For example, you may want to practice some of the Self-Talk for Building Self-Esteem, Determination and Willpower, or Setting and Reaching Goals. When you use this additional Self-Talk, not only are you giving your self the means to deal with the problem, but you are working at changing some of the things that may have *caused* the problem for you in the first place.

TWENTY-ONE

SELF-TALK FOR JOB, CAREER, AND MANAGEMENT

In the first sixty years of life, each of us will spend approximately twenty years growing up, twenty years sleeping (which amounts to eight hours a night for sixty years), and twenty years working. I suspect that our twenty years of "working" are perhaps either the most rewarding—or most frustrating—twenty years of all.

What we do in our careers plays a role in and affects almost everything about how the rest of the hours in our lives go for us. Our work affects our marriage or personal relationships, our families, our friends, what kind of homes we have, how much spare time we have and what we do with it, and, eventually, how we will spend the so-called "retirement" years of our lives—when we are supposed to be able to lie back and enjoy the benefits of what our preceding hard work has created for us.

Meanwhile, while we are on the job, our work—our career—will determine to a great extent how fulfilled we are as individuals, how we greet the day as we get ready to go to the place where we spend a third of our time daily, or how we feel when we come home at night.

On any occasions when I am able to meet and talk to people whom I have not met before, I ask the question "What do you do?" I have been surprised at the number of people who tell me first about their occupation, and then proceed to tell me what they would *like* to be doing—if only they *could*. What interests me most is that the majority could be doing exactly what they *would* really like to do, *if they made the decision to do so.*

CREATING SELF-TALK FOR PERSONAL, PROFESSIONAL, AND FINANCIAL SUCCESS

If you are not happy with your job or career path, you will probably change it. So I have included a script of Self-Talk that will help you with your decision. But the rest of the Self-Talk in this chapter creates the tools to make any career path better. There is Self-Talk for creating more financial freedom, managing the money you earn; some good words about risk; Self-Talk for people in sales; and some excellent Self-Talk for managing others, making decisions, and perfecting your professional "style."

IMPROVING YOUR CAREER

I can think of no time when we need self-confidence more than when changing jobs or making a change in the direction of our careers.

These are often times of indecision and insecurity. The future holds no promises—other than perhaps the promises you make to your self. It is your own attitude and determination that will see you through—and give you the best chance to make it work.

I enjoy seeking and finding new opportunities in my life.

I see every change in my job or career as an opportunity to achieve my goals. I have a positive self-image and I feel good about my self. I am clear, calm, confident, and in control.

I have self-worth and value. I know that I am worthy of succeeding at anything I do, and I deserve the rewards which my achievement brings to me.

I am always aware of my talents, my skills, and my capabilities.

An accurate description of me would include the words "strong," "competent," "qualified," "accomplished," "self-confident," and "capable."

I know that I can accomplish anything I choose in my life. But I also know that it is entirely up to me, and I rely on no one else to accomplish my goals for me. I determine the path which is best for me, I set my goals, and I go for it!

I alone am in control of my life, my self, my thoughts, and my actions. My life is my own, and I accept the responsibility for my success.

I keep my attitude up at all times. I think only those thoughts that are positive, productive, encouraging, and motivating.

I never allow the word "no" to stop me or even slow me down. I say yes to my self, and that's what counts.

I assess my skills often, and I always make sure I have the necessary new skills to meet the career opportunities which are in front of me.

I never allow my self to become tied down to any job or career path which is not genuinely beneficial to me.

I choose not to live my life by the dictates, the demands, or the persuasion of others. My choice is my own, and I know what I want. The path I follow is always my own.

I make sure that my loved ones understand my direction, my objectives, my needs, and my commitment. Their understanding and support create extra drive and enthusiasm within me.

I have determination. I know that nothing can stop me unless I stop my self. So I keep my self in forward motion at all times.

I look forward and never look back. I am busy creating a bright, positive, successful future for my self. I know where I am going, and I am well on my way.

If you are contemplating a change in your job or career, I also recommend that you use some other Self-Talk scripts that help: Believing In Incredible You, Positive Risk-Taking, Personal Achievement, and Freedom from Worry.

A great deal of what happens *to* you in the future will be a direct result of the picture you create of your self in your subconscious mind. It is *always* up to you to create the image of the success that you want. When you are making a change in your job or your career, now is the best time to talk to your self, some of the most positive, confident Self-Talk you have ever used.

POSITIVE RISK-TAKING

It is interesting that there is no "positive" description in our language for the word "risk." And yet without risk there would be no advancement, no progress, no personal growth.

This Self-Talk looks at *positive* risk as a blessing—an opportunity to forge ahead, cover new ground, and create new rewards.

I have the courage to do what I need to do to get where I want to go.

I reduce my risks in taking risks by learning all that I can in advance. Then, having made the decision to move forward, I take each step with the positive decision to succeed.

My path is the bright road of sunlight and promise. And I walk my path with cheerful anticipation. When I take a risk that I know I must, I look forward, expect the best, and never look back.

I have faith in my self and belief in my dreams. I have the capacity to accomplish any objective which I set for my self.

I turn risks and chances into well-planned strategies that favor my success.

For me a good risk is the first stage of a reward. It is a bridge to my success and a doorway to greater opportunity.

I have a good attitude about risks. I see them as a positive part of any achievement, and I accept them with the absolute certainty of my ability to meet and surpass them.

I balance each risk I take with a well-thought-out plan for meeting it. I reduce each risk to steps in a plan of action and ensure my self of the most positive outcome.

I see taking risks as part of the price I am willing to pay for the many benefits and rewards I receive in exchange.

Because I know that risks often represent opportunities to me, my attitude about them is always careful, positive, and constructive.

I am always willing to accept those risks which are necessary for the fulfillment of my goals.

The risks I take are good risks. They always create for me the rewards I seek and they always carry with them continued healthiness and well-being.

Any risk which I accept is a healthy new force in my life. It is a challenge and a worthwhile goal—and another new win in the making.

I accept only those risks which serve to create within me even more positive energy and good in my life and in the lives of those who are important to me.

Each time I read or hear these words I become even more aware of the opportunities which come to me, and I reaffirm my determination to create within them the greatest possible good.

FINANCIAL FREEDOM

There seems to be an unwritten rule that we only earn— or hold on to—what we *think* we deserve. Your *net* worth will average out just as high or just as low as your *self*-worth.

When you begin to increase the value you place on your self, you begin to increase the *potential* of your income; there is a direct cause-and-effect relationship between how you think and what you get.

The man or woman who believes that he or she is destined to live in financial stress ends up in almost every case living a life of limited financial success. The person who *knows* that he deserves more of what life has to offer almost always finds himself earning more.

The process of improving your earnings and building financial freedom starts with several "conditions":

> *1. Agree with your self that it is okay to earn what you would truly like to earn—and accept the fact that you deserve to earn it.*

> *2. Agree with your self that money—or the benefits it can create—is good, worthwhile, and a natural result of your efforts.*

> *3. Agree with your self that you are willing to work for what you get. There is almost never any long-term financial reward without long-term commitment and hard work. "Overnight millionaire" stories are usually just that—stories—and few of them reveal the final chapter.*

> *4. Agree with your self that you are willing to manage the money you earn once you have it.*

Most of us *can* have more financial freedom than we may have allowed our selves to accept in the past. To turn financial worries into peace of mind, perhaps nothing is standing in your way but your beliefs about your self.

I am successful! I am well on my way to even greater financial achievement and independence.

Money comes easily to me. It is one of the rewards I receive for a job well done. And I do all of my jobs well.

I see money as a powerful and positive tool with which I am able to accomplish many good and worthwhile things in my life and in the lives of others.

Financial freedom is just one of the measurements by which I judge my progress toward many of my important professional goals. It is one of the grades I give my self on my "Success Report Card"—and I always make good grades.

Money does for me what I want it to. Money is the servant—I am its master. I do not work for money—money works for me.

I always do, without delay, everything I need to do to achieve the financial goals which I have set for my self.

I enjoy the financial independence which I achieve by meeting my income goals. The more specific and detailed my goal plan is, the faster I achieve each goal and the more financially independent I become.

Each day I become more secure and free from worry and self-doubt. Each day, the achievement of my financial goals comes easier to me.

I believe that my success as a "total" person in mind, body, and spirit is the true measure of my success. Wealth and material gain are important to me for the freedom which they offer me in the pursuit of my ultimate achievements.

I never see money, or material wealth, as being any more important than it actually is. I understand the role it plays in my life, and I keep its role in perspective and in balance.

I am financially responsible. I live my life in a way that assures me of always having extra reserves for unexpected problems or opportunities.

I believe that financial independence and the freedom it gives me are good.

I do not believe that wealth and riches are reserved for a select few—but that life's abundance is available to anyone and everyone who creates it.

Abundance comes to me not by accident, but by design. I am worthy of my achievements and my rewards. I choose them, I visualize them, I create them, I work for them, and I willingly accept them.

I create financial independence in my life in many ways. I set specific goals which tell me exactly how much I will receive, how I will earn it, and when it will come to me.

I visualize each of my financial goals in my mind every day. And I see myself achieving, and deserving, the goals I set.

I enjoy life and its many riches and rewards. *I am good for life—and life is good for me!*

MANAGING MONEY

The goal of the preceding Self-Talk is to create a stronger awareness of the financial freedom you can have in life and to prepare you to get it. Believing you *deserve* financial freedom—in this particular case, having money—and *managing* it when you have it are two different things.

The Self-Talk in this script is specifically about *managing* money. It makes no difference whether you have a lot of money now or not; the kind of money manager you become will determine how much of your earnings you will hold on to, and what they will do for you.

We all have to deal with money. Earning money is one of the reasons we work as hard at our jobs or careers as we do. It is a resource that makes life better for us and for our families. Money can be a valuable resource if we learn how to manage it well. The difference between the "haves" and the "have-nots" has a lot more to do with how well each *manages* money than how *much* they earn.

Our old self-talk about money often says, *"I just can't seem to get ahead"; "I spend more than I make"; "I never have anything left over at the end of the month"; "Money goes through my fingers like water"; "I can never seem to get my bills paid on time"; "I try to budget but I just can't stick with it"; "I'm always a day late and a dollar short"; "It seems like I'm always broke"; "I can never afford the things I want"; or "I just don't know where my money goes."* This kind of self-talk *guarantees* money *mis*management!

Here is a better kind of Self-Talk that will make you aware of how to take care of your money, and help you see your self as a better money manager.

I manage money well. I have a healthy respect for what I earn and what I have—and I make the *most* of it.

I am consciously aware of every dollar I spend, and where I spend it.

I am able to manage money well because I am a good *Self*-Manager. By managing my *self* well, I also manage my *resources* well—and that includes money.

Because I take good care of money—money takes good care of me.

I take the management of my finances seriously. I create for my self the security and the opportunities that I want by managing my money well.

I plan how I will use every dollar I have. I keep a budget and I follow it. I *always* earn more than I spend, and I *never* spend more than I plan.

I manage credit well, and I never misuse it. I am willing to wait for the things which I want. I never feel that I have to have everything *now.*

I never spend money foolishly. I have learned the value of spending wisely. I am thrifty and moderate in all my financial decisions.

I am never impulsive, nor do I feel I have to buy something just because it is something I would like to have.

I never feel the need to *spend* money just because I have money. Every dollar I have now has a *purpose* and is important to me.

I really enjoy the personal satisfaction I get from being good at managing money.

Each day I consciously work at building an even stronger financial future for me and for my loved ones.

Because I manage money well, I am always able to save some of what I earn. I set monthly and yearly savings goals and I meet them.

When I invest money, I invest wisely. I make sure that my money is working for me in the best possible way.

Each day I am becoming a better money manager than ever before. I am in control of my self, my habits, my decisions, and what I do with the money I earn.

I am good at managing money!

There are many other Self-Talk scripts that will help put you in control of your money. People sometimes spend money needlessly because of some *other* problem they are having. Some do it because they are depressed and want to feel better. Others spend more than they should because they want to impress other people. Many people spend out of *habit*. And, of course, many poor money-management choices are made simply because of a lack of good, solid financial goals.

If you want to control how you spend your money, it will help if you can also control other areas that could be creating the problem of overspending. It is very encouraging to know that managing money is a habit and a skill that *anyone*, with the right practice and determination, can learn.

SELF-TALK FOR SALESPEOPLE

I have written and recorded a dozen Self-Talk cassettes designed solely for the demands of the selling "battleground." Salespeople endure huge amounts of rejection; some days, the most frequent word they hear is "no."

Salespeople can, however, prepare themselves to deal with those pressures by paying special attention to their own Self-Talk. There is Self-Talk for Making Sales Presentations, Overcoming Objections, Preparing for Cold Calls, Prospecting for Clients, Maintaining a Winning Attitude, and many other Self-Talk areas too numerous to describe in this book.

The following Self-Talk will give you the idea. It will help you start using the right kind of Self-Talk for selling.

I am very successful at selling. I enjoy selling and I enjoy the many rewards which my success brings to my life.

My selling skills are tops. I am a professional salesperson—and it shows!

I begin each day with a clear mind and a specific plan to get the most from my time and my effort. Each day I follow my plan. Because I do, I reach my goals.

I have mastered the art of getting more done in less time. I am always organized and in control.

I am always on time. And I always save time by planning ahead and allowing extra time for unexpected delays.

I always spend exactly the right amount of time prospecting for more sales. Creating new business comes naturally and easily to me.

An accurate description of me would include the words "professional," "hard working," "qualified," "skillful," "energetic," "enthusiastic," "organized," "determined," and "highly successful."

As a professional salesperson I am always prepared. I take the time to do it right. In everything I do, everyone can see that I am prepared, confident, self-assured, and successful.

I always take care of the details of my work. I enjoy the details

of selling and I always tend to them on time and with full attention.

I keep my self up. I know that making good sales presentations means keeping my self energetic and in control.

My sales presentations are always professional and effective.

I am always sincere and honest. I believe that all success in selling begins with trust, skill, sincerity, and determination.

I never avoid making a sales call of any kind. I keep working, and that keeps me winning.

Being told no never bothers me. Hearing the word "no" doubles my determination and adds to my positive enthusiasm.

I take selling seriously, but I also enjoy it and have fun with it. I really enjoy the freedom and the rewards of selling. And I am one of the best!

MANAGING OTHERS

The Self-Talk in this script talks to you about your skill as a manager. And it also talks to you about your interest in, and support of, the people you manage. The better *they* are, the better *you* are—and vice versa.

Over the years I have met and known managers at every level and station of management responsibility and skill. In every case the *best* managers were always the ones who *saw themselves as professional managers*—not just doing a job, not just putting in a day's work for a day's wage, but *managing,* in the most professional sense of the word.

It did not make any difference how many people they managed or what the job was. They took upon themselves the *responsibility* to care for, support, develop, get the best from, and reward the people they managed. To them, "management" was not a "job"—it was a part of who they were.

There is no one attribute that makes a person a good manager. Management requires the best of a great many skills. To be a good manager of people you need an in-depth knowledge of your product, service, or message; and the skills of organization, sensitivity, time management, training, perseverance, showmanship, motivation, patience, belief, and fortitude.

But to be a good manager, first you have to see your self *being* the person who can handle all that. If you are a manager—whether parent, group coordinator, team leader or business professional, or in any other capacity—my hat is off to you.

Taking upon your self the responsibility to direct, motivate, encourage, depend upon, and then reward the activities of others is a sometimes selfless task which deserves a reward in itself.

Let this Self-Talk offer you some reassurance. I have often thought about the question "Who motivates the motivator?" Who recognizes the job that real managers do? Along with being a good manager, you may, from time to time, also have to be your own best motivator. Here are some of the words you should remember to give your self.

I am a good manager. I manage others well because I manage my self well.

I am organized and on top of the details of my life.

I am in control of my self at all times and in all circumstances.

I take full responsibility for my self. And when I am managing, I allow others to take responsibility for themselves.

I am supportive, understanding, and encouraging. I inspire others to do and to become the very best that they can.

I help others see themselves and their work in the very best way possible. I take the time to show them their qualities and their skills.

I am an excellent communicator. I have learned the art of listening—and I always listen with a clear, receptive mind.

I speak to those I manage with respect and understanding. And I always communicate clearly and directly.

I always look for and find the best in anyone I manage, and I let them know it in a positive way. Because I expect the best from others, I always get it.

People know they can expect fairness from me. I care about them and it shows.

The people I manage always know where they stand with me. I am open, honest, and sincere with my self and with them.

I have a good attitude about my self and about the people I work with. They enjoy the opportunity to work with me—and I really enjoy working with them.

I recognize the job that I do, and I take the time to reward my self for a job well done!

I have learned that managing others is a reflection of how I manage my self. Being a good manager is one of the many rewarding successes of my life.

Each day I work to improve my management skills and to become an even better manager than ever before.

I am a good manager!

MAKING DECISIONS

Every one of us, like it or not, lives a life of making decisions. That's the way it ought to be, of course; the alternative is to live a life in which decisions are taken care of by someone else. Most of us would rather make at least some of our decisions by ourselves, no matter how difficult it might be.

"Making decisions" goes far beyond having to make important decisions of life; it has to do with making *choices* for ourselves in the largest and the smallest areas of our lives.

Every movement you make tomorrow—or any day

thereafter—will be governed by the decisions you make now. Few of them will be major. Most will be incidental. But all, either consciously or unconsciously, will require some decision making on your part.

The right to make your own decisions is one of the greatest rights you will ever have. But like so many subjects we have discussed that have to do with "self-betterment," decision making is a skill most of us were never taught in school.

I'm not talking only about the kinds of decisions business people are trained to make; I'm also talking about the everyday decisions of life. We learn to make them—or avoid them—almost *accidentally* by being conditioned by others.

THE DECISIONS YOU MAKE ARE YOUR CHOICES IN LIFE

Everything you do is the result of decisions you make. All of us make dozens of decisions in a single day—most of which we are not even aware of making. And yet every one affects you in some way. If you are aware of them, you give your self more *choice* in the matter. By recognizing that your decisions are the directions that plot the course of your life, you give your self the chance to decide what you want those decisions to be.

One of the treasures you were given at birth was the *right,* and the *responsibility,* to make decisions for your self. If you give away that right you will always have to live with the results of allowing the rest of the world to make decisions for you.

It is easy sometimes to get the feeling that life is a spectator sport: We are watching a game, played by others whom we allow to make *our* decisions—and somehow control or play out *our* lives for us. Meanwhile, we begin to believe that our own lives—our "selves"—are not at risk. The batter steps up to the mound and hits the ball—or he misses. The quarterback makes a split-second decision to throw the ball or make a run for the last five yards. We are watching the game, but someone else is playing it for us.

But the life you live every day does *not* have to be a spectator sport. *You* are the player, and you have the option to play the game. If you make your own decisions, chances are good that you will live your life in a way that gives you more happiness and fulfillment.

Your decisions do not always have to be right. Everyone makes mistakes along the way. But you, your life, and every part of it will fare better if you make the decision to make your own decisions. This doesn't mean you should not get good advice or accept intelligent input from someone else. But when it comes down to it, the world becomes a better place to live when you are in control of yourself, and enjoying the freedom of making your own decisions.

I make good decisions. I trust in my judgment and I have faith in my self and in my abilities.

I take the time to think through any decision I make. But when something needs to be done, I get it done. So I make good decisions rapidly and on time.

I never put off making any decision that I need to make. I set my priorities and I make the decisions that put my plans into action!

I enjoy the satisfaction I receive from making good decisions and getting things done.

I organize my thoughts. I am able to see alternative solutions clearly and accurately. I assess the situation, select the right course of action, and make the right decision.

I am open and objective. I am good at bringing together the facts I need—to make the very best decision I can make.

I spend no time giving unnecessary thought to worrying about the outcome of the decisions I have made. I spend my time making my decisions work, in the most positive and productive way.

I never allow the fear of failure to stand in the way of making a decision. I look instead at the positive, successful outcome of any decision I make.

If I make a mistake, I am always able to see it in the very best way, correct it, and move on.

I have confidence in my self. I seek, and listen to, the counsel and advice of others, but I also listen to the counsel of my own mind.

I know that my successes are the positive result of the decisions I make, both in my personal life and in my professional life.

I may rely on the help and support that others give, but I never require or allow other people to make my decisions for me.

I know that I alone am responsible for my choices, my decisions, and my actions—in every area of my life. I take full responsibility for every decision I make.

I look forward, each day, to the opportunity to practice my skills in making good decisions. I manage my self and my decisions well.

POLISHING PROFESSIONAL "STYLE"

Professional "style" means how we handle our selves on the job (and off), every day and throughout our careers. There are few schools or colleges that teach us how to act on the job—how to think, what to say or not say, how to dress, or how to create an *internal* style that ends up creating career "success" for us.

The person who wants a high level of success would find that most of the Self-Talk scripts in this book apply. The Self-Talk of success includes a broad variety of personal objectives. Being successful involves goals, taking personal responsibility, dealing with problems, having strong self-esteem, thinking sharp and being alert and aware, taking action, and learning to take care of the smallest details, while at the same time keeping your eye on the bigger picture—with foresight and perspective.

All of these skills are important—and all of them will help. But they will also help you achieve the success you want by giving you self-directions that tell you very specifically how to put your other Self-Management skills to work. You can apply those same skills *directly* to your goals of becoming, every day, a better professional.

I always visualize my self being at my absolute best in every part of my professional life.

I am a successful professional—and it shows! I am a true professional in my skills, my appearance, my thinking, my actions, and my accomplishments.

I dress well and I look sharp! When people meet me they automatically see me as the polished, successful professional that I am.

I pay attention to even the smallest details of my physical appearance, my manner, my conduct, and my "presence." I always present the best of who I am.

I know that the presentation of my "self" is always the most important presentation I can make. So I make sure that I am organized, in control, looking good, and unmistakably confident.

I never overdo my appearance or style in any way. I am always professionally appropriate, completely in tune, and in touch with the circumstances of any situation.

My posture is positive and strong. I always sit, stand, walk, and move with a natural bearing of individual strength and confidence.

Even my gestures exemplify a strong personal attitude of confidence and capability.

I am always aware of exactly when to speak, when not to speak, and how much to say.

When I speak, I always speak with conviction. I choose my words well; I am articulate, concise, and to the point. People respect this quality in me—and because of it, they listen to what I have to say.

I never embellish the truth or change the facts. I see and present things exactly as they really are.

I am practical and realistic, but I have also learned to phrase my words in the positive. People around me always know that they can count on me for solid, practical ideas and solutions.

I never seek to win the approval of someone by saying yes, when the answer should be no. I stand on the solid ground of my own conviction—at all times, and in all circumstances.

I am never intimidated by others, regardless of their rank or position. I see them instead as individuals who rely on my capabilities and trust my support.

I am good at seeing the broad picture, but I also take care of the smallest details of my work.

I am constantly improving my professional skills and my value as a professional individual.

I never make excuses for my self or my actions. I always work to do my best, and my best is very good.

I am a good team player, but I also function well on my own. I can be counted on, whether I am working by myself or with others.

My decision to be a true professional, every day, in everything that I do, makes the rest of my life work even better for me.

I really enjoy seeing the results of my solid professional style. I have learned the art of mastering the skills that make my career work for me.

I am reliable, capable, organized, hard working, productive, supportive, and successful. I am on top of my job, in touch with my self, and highly professional.

I have known many successful professional people. Whether they were in business or involved in any other organization, the "attitude" of *professionalism* is precisely the Self-Management skill each of them had learned to use. This skill most certainly played a major part in creating the professional success that each achieved.

After a talk I gave at a national sales meeting of a large retail-store chain, the chairman of the board had this response: "If each of our employees and managers would trade in one or two of their old attitudes for *that* kind of Self-Talk— that kind of attitude—we would never have to worry about our competition; our competition would spend their time worrying about *us*."

Your professional polish—your skills, your attitude, your methods, and your style—will *always* have a direct effect on your success. If anyone can play a role in making a more rewarding professional career for your self—it is *you*.

PERSONAL ACHIEVEMENT

This particular Self-Talk script has always been one of my favorites. It is a Self-Talk that reminds us of our higher potential. It restates how capable and fulfilled each of us *can* be—if we just give our selves the chance.

When I tackle a difficult new project, or begin to lose sight of my objective, I play the tape of this script a few times to get myself back on target. It never fails to revitalize my thinking and rekindle my belief in the best of what we humans have to offer.

This one simple Self-Talk script teaches us the kind of self-belief that I wish could be given to every child or adult who has ever struggled with the problems of life or questioned whether he or she had the potential to achieve.

A business executive from California once wrote me about the effect his Self-Talk was having on his business. He wrote: "Anytime I get down or become discouraged, I listen to the cassette on *Believing in Incredible You,* and then I end up by listening to the cassette on *Personal Achievement.* The other Self-Talk helps me motivate my self, but listening to that one tape, more than any other, reminds me of what I'm doing it all for."

I believe the reason so many people have used this Self-Talk script repeatedly over a period of years is that it reveals a part of the "universal truth" which is a part of each of us. I suspect that these words will continue to be a part of my life for many years to come. I hope that you will make them a part of yours.

I am a true achiever—a winner in every sense of the word.

I set my goals and I reach them. Success, for me, is a way of life.

Within me lives an undeniable spirit, an indestructible will, and an unfailing determination to succeed. I know that nothing can still the giant within me, or diminish the light of my dreams.

I know that my success is in the doing as much as in the winning, and that the reward comes to me each day—even while the goal is being sought and long before the goal has been won.

It is not important to me to be the best that there is—it is only important to me to be the best that I can. My goal is not to surpass others, but rather to live up to the best of who I am.

Achieving things that are important to me is rewarding and exciting. But I know that nothing is free. I am willing to pay the price for any achievement which I truly desire.

I know that my goals are worthy of me—and I am worthy of them.

My achievement doesn't happen only at the end of my journey, it happens to me every day in everything I do. I enjoy the day-to-day job of working for my goals just as much as I enjoy the final accomplishment.

I encourage others to do well, but I never demand encouragement from others.

I recognize that the achievement of my goals is my own personal choice—and their accomplishment is up to me. I never

expect others to achieve my goals for me, to take my risks, or to help me pay the price which I have agreed to pay.

I take full responsibility for the achievement of every goal I set.

I am unwilling to sit back, get by, and achieve little. I take full advantage of the talent, the strength, and the potential which I am, even now, bringing to life within me.

I reach my goals and fulfill my dreams by following the specific steps of the plan which I write for them. I never leave achievement up to chance.

I am not afraid to walk new paths or break new ground. Because my expectations are never average, I do not walk the well-worn paths of indifference or mediocrity. Instead, I follow the paths of my own choosing.

I have all of the ingredients in the formula for living my life in the very best way—and I put them to work for me. I have the vision to see the objective. I have the plan, and I follow it. And I have the spirit to work as hard as necessary to get the job accomplished.

I refuse to accept any limitations to my personal achievement which others may try to place on me. I live my life by my own design, and not by the disbeliefs or the limitations of others.

I have made the decision to become the very best of who I am. That is how I choose to be. That is how I choose to live my life.

TWENTY-TWO

SELF-TALK FOR A *MENTAL* "TUNE-UP"

The Self-Talk in this chapter helps you fine-tune your mind to get it working right, and to be focused when you need to be at your *best*.

Use this Self-Talk when you have an important job (or obstacle) in front of you, and your thoughts need to be crystal clear and your confidence high. Whether you are a salesperson, a student, have to speak in front of a group, or are going for a job interview, you can help put your self at your best—in advance.

Keep in mind that many of your new directives are replacing or overriding old programs that have told you the *wrong* things about your self in the past. Whether you want to open your self up to being more creative, to focus your attention, or to retain more of what you are learning, you will *always* improve your chances by giving your self the right directions.

Many people use this Self-Talk as a mental warmup for facing important situations. It may not change your entire attitude overnight; that takes longer. But it will *temporarily* help you gear up for the challenge before you while it begins to work at creating some long-term changes.

THINKING SHARP AND BEING ALERT

You have probably had days when you needed to be at your best mentally, and it was a real effort to clear out the cobwebs and get on track. I have had days like that. But I have learned that there are ways to make the jump from being unclear to *sharp* in no more than a few minutes.

The following is an example of one of those Self-Talk scripts that have an effect right now—today. It doesn't take weeks of repetition and practice to see results.

Anytime you have to be especially alert and aware, just focus your attention, give your self strong, immediate self-commands to concentrate, listen to what you are telling your self, and follow the directions that your Self-Talk is giving you.

I am alert and aware. My senses are keen and sharp. My mind is clear. I am in touch with everything around me and in control of my life.

My thinking is especially sharp today. I see things with great clarity. Understanding comes easily and naturally to me today.

Even my intuition is more sensitive and aware than ever before. Both my conscious and my unconscious minds are perfectly tuned to the world around me. I feel completely confident and in step with my life.

My mind is clear and alert, and it is capable of meeting any challenge I place before it.

My imagination is especially useful to me. The pictures in my mind are vivid and sharp. I see details clearly, and I am able to visualize anything I choose to see.

My concentration is finely tuned and focused. I am in complete control of my thoughts. I do not have to spend time clearing my head or waking my senses. I am instantly alert and aware, anytime I need to be.

I look forward with positive enthusiasm to opportunities which test and improve my mental alertness. Instead of seeing problems as difficulties to be avoided, I see them as opportunities to sharpen my mental skill and agility.

I use my mind well. I keep my mental equipment in good condition. I exercise my mind daily, and I look for opportunities to strengthen and improve my mind in everything that I do.

I think only those thoughts which are of benefit to me and which serve to create the greatest possible good. My mind is a finely tuned instrument which works for me in the most positive possible way.

I know that my mind works for me because I tell it what to do. I never leave the programming or the directing of my mind up to chance. I accept the responsibility to consciously program my mind daily with specific, positive directives and directions.

Each day I nourish and improve my mind. I read to expand the knowledge I need. I listen to improve my understanding of the thoughts of others.

Every time I speak, I practice articulating my ideas with ever-increasing clarity and effectiveness.

Each day I become more alert, mentally effective, and in control.

Each day my own mind becomes an even more powerful mechanism which works for me for the achievement of my goals.

I would also recommend that when you use this Self-Talk, you follow it up with Self-Talk for Improving Your Concentration and if the situation calls for it, add the Self-Talk for Memory. Someone once said, "A clear, sharp, organized mind is the product of a clear, sharp, organized mind."

There is no better place to start the process of having a clear, sharp, organized mind than your own Self-Talk.

SPEAKING AND WRITING WITH CONFIDENCE

How effective you are on the job or off will often depend on how well you express your self. How well you do this will depend not only on the skills you learn, it will depend on the internal attitude you have about expressing your self.

If you would like to improve your skills of being an articulate, confident speaker, presenter, or writer, add a well-trained *attitude* to the rest of your training.

I have good thoughts and good ideas, and I am able to express my thoughts and ideas to others in a clear and interesting way.

I speak clearly because I think clearly. I think clearly because I concentrate on only one subject at a time.

Because I know how to think, I know what to think. Knowing how to think, and how to direct my own thoughts, make it easy for me to know what to say.

When I speak or write, I follow the rule of simplicity. I speak and write simply and directly.

People like the way I express my self, and they enjoy hearing my thoughts and ideas.

My mind gives me the words I need, exactly when I need them.

I am an interesting speaker because I think good, positive, helpful, interesting thoughts. I am creative. I have many good ideas. And I enjoy expressing my ideas to others.

I never speak or write to impress others. "Expression," not "impression," is the key to getting my ideas across.

When I speak and when I write, I paint clear, simple pictures with my words.

Each day I express my ideas more clearly. My mind is organized. I know what I think, and I express my self clearly, simply, and sincerely.

Each day my confidence in my self-expression grows stronger and even more positive. I express myself easily, without fear or uncertainty.

In every opportunity I have to communicate with others, I am decisive, direct, warmly received—and effective!

IMPROVING YOUR CONCENTRATION

Just as we discussed in the section on Self-Talk for Thinking Sharp and Being Alert, this Self-Talk script is the kind that goes to work almost as soon as you begin using it.

Professionals in some of the most demanding occupations rely on this Self-Talk to create instant focus and alertness. Few of us realize, for example, that when we are in an airplane, the pilot flying that plane has more than likely been trained in the use of precisely this form of Self-Talk. During the final, critical minutes of landing a commercial airline jet, the captain will often repeat specific Self-Talk statements *out loud* as a normal part of his landing procedure.

A letter I received from an airline flight instructor about his own success with Self-Talk proved just how specific Self-Talk can get. He wrote: "We use it to teach pilots to fly better. Instead of their saying, 'My altitude is off 50 feet,' they say, 'I'm on altitude.' Instead of 'I've lost an engine,' they say, 'I've got it under control; my heading and altitude are stable; I'll find the problem soon.' When they're on a tricky instrument approach, they say, 'This is a piece of cake; I'm on localizer; I'm on glidescope; I'm on airspeed.' " And he concluded with "It works."

You may not be responsible for bringing a Boeing 747 loaded with passengers safely into Kennedy Airport, but there are times when the same attention to concentration can help you, too. Whether you are doing a difficult job at work, studying for a test, or even just listening intently to what someone is saying, the same self-directions apply.

When you need to concentrate, practice the following

Self-Talk—and follow it up with some specific, direct-to-the-point Self-Talk of your own.

I have excellent powers of concentration. In my mind I am able to become a part of the subject I am concentrating on.

When I concentrate, I attune ALL of my senses to the subject at hand, and I am able to focus my attention more and more easily each day.

I practice the art of tuning in to the subject I am concentrating on. When I give something my attention, I am able to give it my COMPLETE attention.

Each day I consciously work to improve and perfect my ability to direct and hold my concentration.

I am able, by my own self-direction, to unite my senses, bring all of my awareness into focus, and aim the energy of my attention in one direction for as long as I require.

When I am concentrating or studying, my mind never drifts. Instead, it stays on the subject; it is crystal-clear and locked in to the direction and subject which I choose.

I am in complete control of the concentration of my own mind. I direct its attention and I command its thoughts.

My mind automatically blocks out any distractions—both from within and without—which are not really important to me.

I have patience. Maintaining my concentration, even for long periods of time, comes naturally to me.

Each day my thinking skills become even more finely tuned, and I look forward to opportunities for me to develop my thinking and concentration skills. I practice targeting my attention, focusing my thoughts, and maintaining full control over my mind.

My mind responds positively and enthusiastically to the idea of "study." Because of this, anything I choose to study or learn is openly received and welcomed by my mind.

When I want to concentrate quickly and completely, I give my mind three key words, which immediately focus my mental energy. The key words are "picture," "target," and "focus." Each time I need to concentrate, I say these three words aloud or to myself.

I like to concentrate. And the more I use this important skill of consciously focusing my attention—the easier it becomes.

STUDYING AND LEARNING

How much better we might fare if we never had a problem with studying or learning. I know that my own days in school, and many times since, could have gone much easier for me.

Studying and learning are both habits. We learn to study and we learn to learn. They are habits that are affected by the *attitudes* we have with us. The following sample of Self-Talk is not a short course in study habits, it is a short course about learning in general. The more enthusiastically you approach any learning process you undertake, the better you will do.

I am always learning something new. I feel good about the skills I already have, and I work to create even greater competence in everything I do.

I am alert and aware, and every day I look forward to learning something new.

I have many talents and I use them well. I develop my talents, and I use them to create good for my self and for others.

I explore new interests in my mind which hold new and untapped talents within me. I look for and find new talents within me because I know that they represent new growth and potential in my future.

Learning is the gold that I place in the bank of my mind. And I invest in my self every day.

I am completely open to the idea of learning new things. Learning comes naturally to me. I never stop learning, and I enjoy the satisfaction that it gives me. The more I learn, the more I live.

Other people see me as interesting, aware, and resourceful. Learning new things helps to keep me that way.

Each time I write goals for my self and for my future, I make sure they include specific new skills and talents which I want to develop in my self.

I am capable of learning anything I choose.

When I am confronted by a roadblock that stands between me and my learning, I meet the challenge, overcome it, and learn more because of it.

I like to learn. It is interesting, fun, and it keeps me aware and in touch. Learning makes me feel good about my self.

I practice good study habits. The way I study makes learning come easier to me now.

When I study, I study! I concentrate my thoughts, focus my energies, and pay attention to what I am learning.

I never put studying off or avoid any responsibility that is mine. I get my work done on time and in the right way.

The more I practice studying, the more I enjoy it. And I especially like the benefits that studying and learning are creating in my life.

MEMORY

Have you ever heard someone say, "I have a poor memory," or "I have the world's *worst* memory"? How's *that* for some powerful programming? It instructs the person saying it to be exactly the *opposite* of the way he would like to be!

A skilled, reliable memory can do wonders for you in almost any area of your life. If you would like to experience a better memory you may choose to enroll in a course that teaches memory skills—but *start* by learning new self-directions about your own memory, and the natural capability that is already a part of you.

I have a good memory.

Because my mind is alert and aware, my memory is clear and my recall is excellent.

I never have trouble remembering names or faces. I am interested in the people I meet—and it shows!

I take advantage of books on memory improvement. I read these books, practice them, and I use their ideas daily.

I have embarked on a lifelong program of mental fitness. This adds to my self-confidence and makes me more determined to improve my memory skills even more.

I tell my self every day, and in every situation it applies, that I have an excellent memory. I frequently tell my self the words "I always remember names," and "I always remember anything I want to remember."

I often give my self the self-direction "Remember this" when I encounter any detail, name, or fact which I want to recall clearly later. When my mind hears the words "Remember this," I automatically add energy and emphasis to my memory programming, and it works—I remember it!

I constantly practice new memory-building techniques to improve my mental skills.

I take special note of things throughout each day which I want to remember later—and I practice remembering these things

and bringing them back to my mind easily and clearly, anytime I choose.

I use the technique of mentally taking a snapshot of specific situations and making a "print" of the snapshot in my mind.

I always clearly remember conversations I have with others. I am able to recall important comments word for word. This helps me in my work and in all areas of my life.

One reason I remember conversations so completely and clearly is that I always LISTEN completely and clearly.

A good memory is the product of an organized and well-trained mind. That describes my mind perfectly.

Mastering my own memory is very important to me. Each day improving my alertness, my attention, and my memory comes easier to me.

CREATIVITY

In my years of attempting to understand the workings of human behavior, I have come across few human qualities that have been as misunderstood as individual "creativity."

Most researchers and behavioral scientists agree that creativity is *natural:* We are *born* creative! And yet I meet so many people who tell me, "I'm just not creative," or "I couldn't do that; I'm just not creative enough."

Creativity appears to be a part of us which, all too often, is somehow trained *out* of us—usually during childhood. You possess, at this moment and at all times, more natural creative ability than you could ever use. It makes no difference what your career is, what your education or background are; your own creativity is, if you allow it to be, a natural, everyday part of you.

The question is not whether you can be more creative. The question is only whether you will *allow* your self to exercise the creativity you already have.

Creativity is not limited to producing great works of art

or literature. Creativity is one of the single most important driving forces that guide, direct, and bring to life every goal or accomplishment. And you can begin putting more of it to use the moment you recognize you already have it.

I am creative. I like to find new and interesting ways to think and do things in my life.

I like new ideas. I enjoy being innovative, and I like to create new and better ways to solve problems and deal with life's situations.

I do not believe that creativity is reserved for others. I do not see creativity as a gift which is given solely to so-called creative people. I see creativity as a natural part of each of us which can be developed and enhanced in anyone.

I see my own creativity as the key which unlocks my true potential.

An accurate description of the real me would include the words "resourceful," "inventive," "innovative," "willing to try new ideas," "imaginative," and "very creative."

I am becoming more creative with each new day. I realize that the only limits on my creativity were the limits which I placed on my self in the past. I now choose to place no limits on my creativity at any time or for any reason.

I admire and respect others who use their own imaginations in ways which benefit themselves and others. And I know that others see me and respect me as a very creative, resourceful individual.

I am not afraid to try the untried, walk new paths, or search for new and better alternatives in every detail and part of my life.

I never try to be different for the sake of difference itself. But I am never afraid to be different when my own creative imagination shows me a better path to follow.

I am a new person today. I accept none of the limitations I placed on my own imagination yesterday. Today I am more creative than ever before.

My own creativity enables me to unlock the source from which all ideas flow. I ask the question and the answers come to me. I state the problem and my creative mind leads me on the path to its solution.

Since my imagination knows no limits, my creativity has no bounds.

The more I practice using my creative mind, the more creative I become. The more creative I am, the more successful I am in everything that I do.

VISUALIZATION

I was interviewed recently by a writer preparing an article for a leading magazine aimed at weight-conscious people. She asked me for several Self-Talk phrases on losing weight that she could include in her article. I was amazed when she told me that the editors of the magazine did not want me to suggest any Self-Talk on "visualization"—the kind of Self-Talk that would help the reader have a mental "picture" of *being* slim.

Visualization is as important to Self-Talk as a stage setting is to a Broadway play. It is by *seeing* your self in a new way, a new setting, with all the details in place that you show your subconscious mind what you want it to do for you. Visualizing is the best way we have of saying to the subconscious, "See this picture? *That's* what I want!"

I frequently receive calls during radio talk shows from people who tell me that they cannot visualize things easily. While some people are blessed with an internal motion-picture projector that literally creates mental pictures in 3-D, others have trouble creating visual images easily and clearly.

Motivational trainers often recommend that we cut out pictures of our "goals" from magazines and tape them to the bathroom mirror—to help us *mentally* visualize the goals.

During the last few years, research in mind-brain function has proved that our mental pictures play a vital part in the future we create for our selves. Learning how to be a good visualizer is proving to be one of the most important skills in creating who we are, what we do, and how well we do it.

A well-trained salesperson, for example, will rehearse his presentation repeatedly, not only to perfect his selling skill, but to practice *visualizing* in advance every step of a *successful* presentation so clearly in his mind that the final outcome will duplicate that picture.

The Self-Talk in the following script will help you if visualizing has been difficult for you. It also will help you visualize *more*—more often, more clearly, and more effectively—even if you are already able to create, and *see,* your own future successes in your mind.

I have learned to picture my own successes—in *advance*—in my mind.

I am able to visualize pictures and events clearly in my mind, and each time I do this it becomes easier.

I improve my visualization by practicing seeing simple, everyday objects in my mind. I practice seeing them clearly and accurately.

I have learned to visualize a single object in my mind and ask my self to literally *"see"* its shape, its size, its color, and even the smallest details of its makeup.

Each day I frequently practice concentrating my attention and focusing it for a moment on one picture in my mind. This helps me visualize easily and naturally anytime I choose.

I also practice seeing my self in the pictures in my mind. And I make sure that I always see my self looking, acting, and being the way I really want to be.

I create complete detailed scenes in my mind of my self in successful situations. I see these scenes over and over, each time

more clearly, and I begin to create that future event in my
mind.

When visualizing my self in successful situations, I not only *see*
my self, I *feel* my self—even the clothes I am wearing, the room
I'm in, and the emotion I'm feeling.

I know that I begin to create in reality those things I visualize
most in my mind. So I visualize those pictures and scenes
which create the future I want.

Anytime I want to improve the possible outcome of any situation in front of me, I *pre*play my success in advance over and
over.

When I am visualizing a future event, I always see my motions,
hear my words, and feel my success—clearly and consciously.

I create situations in my mind that turn problems into solutions—and I visualize my self making those solutions work.

I turn daydreams into fun, exciting preplays of my future. By
practicing visualizing my self in this way, I literally shape and
create some of the best of my future.

Because I am responsible for every one of my own thoughts,
that means that I am responsible for visualizing the events of
my own future in the most positive possible way.

I enjoy visualizing. I often practice positive visualization when
I am relaxing, and even just before I go to sleep at night.

I not only visualize my self as successful, I also always see my
self being healthy, happy, and having great peace of mind.

Each day I get even better at clearly visualizing the best of my
self and my future in my own mind. I visualize it, I act on it—
and I make it happen.

TWENTY-THREE

SELF-TALK FOR SOLVING PROBLEMS

If you have read this book from the beginning, you already know that most of what we call "problems," have in the past been problems only because we chose to look at them that way. They have, in many cases, been the result of our own programming and our own past self-talk.

The Self-Talk in this chapter deals with problems in a different light. Worry, normal depression, and so-called personal limitations, are seen as natural challenges of everyday living. We *all* have them. But how you look at problems in your life will always depend on your own personal programming. That is why two people, similar in almost every other way, will see their problems in an entirely different way from each other.

I hope you find the Self-Talk in this chapter as encouraging and as uplifting as I have. One of my favorite Self-Talk scripts is the first one in this section, entitled, "Overcoming Personal Limitations." Many people have told me that they have found this group of Self-Talk phrases particularly inspiring—regardless of the size or shape of the problem they were up against.

I also recommend that you use some of the Self-Talk scripts that are in the other chapters. Many of them are designed to help you get your self to *do* something specific— to *take action,* which is one of the best remedies for dealing with problems.

If we live a life of stress because of a problem which cannot be changed, then the real problem is how we *perceive,* on the *inside,* the problem on the *outside.*

OVERCOMING PERSONAL LIMITATIONS

There are times when you face problems that don't come from the outside—they come from the *inside.* Those are the times when self-created limitations get in your way.

You may not be able to override past programming overnight, but you can, in time, rid your self of many self-imposed limitations that have no business taking up space in your mental computer.

Get tough with your self! Tell your self that you no longer accept the limitations you have lived with in the past.

There is nothing which can bind my unconquerable spirit. Nothing can diminish the certainty of my dreams. I have given freedom to my thoughts and wings to my imagination. I have unleashed the unlimited potential which is within me.

I am everything that is—my thoughts, my life, my dreams come true. I am everything I choose to be. I am as unlimited as the endless universe.

I accept none of the limitations which others may try to place on me—they are their limitations, not mine—and they play no part in my destiny.

Each day I consciously remove from my mind the imaginary bindings of self-doubt and the unnecessary limitations of uncertainty and fear.

I daily free my thoughts and energies for the exciting pursuit of my most positive expectations—and for the realization and fulfillment of my dreams.

I believe in my self. I know that I have the power to achieve any goal which I set, and to accomplish any task which is in front of me.

There really is nothing that can stand in the way of my true success. After all, I created my limitations in the first place, and I can take them away.

In my world there are exciting possibilities and unlimited opportunities. I see them, I believe in them, and really enjoy creating them.

When I have a job to do, I spend my time finding ways to get it done and doing it—not creating reasons why I can't.

My rule is: "Don't think about why I cannot—think about how I can."

I believe that anything is possible—unless I believe that it isn't.

I conquer my fears, they do not conquer me. I confront them, I look at them, I understand them, I deal with them, and I defeat them.

By refusing to give faith to my fears, I take their energy from them, and they dissipate in front of me, like wisps of clouds in a clear blue sky.

I replace fear with love and self-assurance. I replace limitations with belief and determination. With a combination like that, I cannot lose.

Life is full of endless, positive possibilities for me, and I am ready to meet every challenge and every opportunity which is presented to me.

As positively as I have conditioned my mind to think, and as prepared for success as I am, my horizons are broader and my skies are brighter than ever.

DEALING WITH PROBLEMS

We have learned that so-called successful people treat problems differently from others. By a change in attitude and perception, what is a "problem" for one person can be a stepping-stone for someone else.

When I meet someone who says life is "full of problems," I usually find that he or she has no more problems than anyone else. But because of past conditioning, that person has gotten into the habit of *seeing* life as being "full of problems."

Any difficult situation you encounter can be looked at either as a normal part of life or as a "problem." The choice of how you look at it is up to you. If you view the normal circumstances of life as problems—you will find a lot of them. If instead you choose to see those same circumstances as signposts telling you that you are alive and well—and in the middle of your journey—then this gives you a better chance of making the *best* of them.

I'm good at solving problems. I like challenges and I meet them head on.

Problems are my teachers. They help me to learn and grow. Without them, I would be going nowhere. With them, I am moving forward in the direction of my goals.

There is no problem which I cannot conquer. I am strong in mind, body, and spirit. My will, my strength, and my determination are always greater than any problem I face.

When I meet a new problem, I do not see the problem as my enemy. I know that finding the solution to a problem will move me forward in my own personal growth.

Because I know that problems are a key ingredient in my spiritual and mental education and preparation, I recognize that all problems are important to me.

I do not fear problems, I solve them. I do not ignore problems, I confront them. I do not avoid problems, I conquer them!

I know that every problem holds within itself the keys to its own solution. Therefore, the better I understand the problem, the clearer I am able to see its solution.

Having problems is not a problem for me. I am confident, self-assured, positive, and determined. I always know that I am going to overcome any problem I encounter—and I always do.

I am good at breaking large obstacles down into smaller pieces that are easier to handle. And I never make any problem appear to be larger than it actually is.

I never worry. I turn "worry time" into positive, constructive "solution time."

I keep my mind alert and open to all solutions—and solutions come quickly and easily to me.

I am not afraid of any problem. I prefer to meet a problem face-to-face. I learn everything I can about the problem, I understand it, define it, and I make a detailed outline of the possible solutions. I arrange the solutions in priority order, and I immediately begin acting on the first step in the list of solutions.

I have learned to recognize that many problems carry with them benefits and potential opportunities which would not have presented themselves, had the problem not occurred in the first place.

I do not seek to live a life which is free from all problems. Instead, I choose to live a life of finding solutions and enjoying the benefits which those solutions create.

"Challenge," "conquer," "solution," and "win" are words I live by daily. "Challenges" are opportunities. "Conquering them" is the inevitable outcome. "Solutions" are stepping-stones to my success, and "winning" is my way of life.

OVERCOMING DEPRESSION

Even minor depression has a way of slowing us down, draining energy, and causing us to lose sight of a more positive side of life.

Some forms of depression are caused by a physical condition and should be treated medically. But most common forms of depression are created by something that has happened in the past, or is happening now, which brings us down, causes us to lose hope, or leads us into despair.

This kind of depression is usually treated with an improved diet, regular exercise, constructive activity, and a concentrated effort to deal with the problems causing the depression. A program that includes each of these "therapies" will almost always help reduce the depression.

However, the *real* cause of this form of depression is *internal*—not *external*. And you can do something about that.

Before you are convinced that there is nothing you can do, give your self the chance to try changing some of those thoughts and feelings that created the depression in the first place.

I believe in my self! I believe that I can achieve anything I choose—and I choose to feel *great!*

I enjoy being active. I am productive and I get things done. Each day I outline my schedule of activities, and I follow my schedule.

I eat exactly the food I need to keep me physically healthy and mentally alert and feeling good.

I know that my diet is important to me, and I enjoy taking proper care of my diet, and daily increasing my healthiness and well-being.

Each day I enjoy being interested in something which is special to me.

I start and end every day with a smile. And throughout each day, I consciously practice smiling and feeling good about my self.

My appearance is important to me. I always keep my self looking great, and that's the way I feel.

I set goals which I can reach every day. By doing this I create a pattern of successes for my self. By being successful each day, I reaffirm my ability to be successful in anything I do.

I take the time to schedule my activities each day. I plan my day and I follow my plan.

I always get the rest and relaxation I need, but I never spend more time resting or sleeping than I should—and I especially enjoy getting up and getting at it!

I think only those thoughts which help me accomplish my most worthwhile goals. My thoughts are always clear, bright, strong, positive, and productive.

As of this moment, and at all other times, I give my self permission to make positive changes in my life. I see the good in everything that is around me, and each day I take the time to recognize the opportunities and the rewards which lie in front of me.

I refuse to allow anything to stop me for long. I pick my self up, dust my self off, hold my chin up, smile, and start walking.

I have learned three magic words which defeat depression and create a brighter day in front of me. The three words are "GET SOMETHING DONE!" . . . and I do!

FREEDOM FROM WORRY

When you worry, it is not because it is human nature for you to do so. Worry is *not* an instinct or a trait you were born with. Worry is a habit; it is learned.

Worry is different from "being concerned." It is *natural* to be concerned about things that threaten you or someone or something important to you. Concern is your mind's way of getting you to take notice and, if necessary, take action.

But healthy concern often turns into unhealthy worry— a form of fear and doubt that all too often exaggerates a problem, makes you dwell on it and replay it over and over in your mind *without* creating a solution.

It has been said that we could conquer most of the problems that plague us if we replaced every moment of worry with an equal amount of "solution," or, if there is no solution, with "acceptance." The truth is, we *can't* solve some of the things that bother us, while we *can* solve others. The solution for worry, as we have often been told, is to do something about those things we *can* change, and learn to accept those things which we cannot.

Learning not to worry does not mean learning to "avoid" problems. Paying attention to the circumstances of your life is essential to Self-Management. But spending your time and precious mental energies *worrying* about things you can do nothing about helps no one, and it can, if worrying goes on long enough, have serious physical consequences.

I like the Self-Talk statement that says, *"I turn 'worry time' into 'action time.' "* Making that one seemingly simple decision can have an effect on your entire attitude toward problems and solutions.

My mind is constantly in tune with the positive—it is bright, cheerful, enthusiastic—and full of good, positive thoughts and ideas.

I am able to relax easily and comfortably in my body and in my mind. I am calm, confident, and self-assured.

My mind is orderly and well organized. I consciously choose what I think, and I always choose those thoughts which are the most positive and beneficial for me.

All of my thoughts create healthiness within me. My mind dwells only on those thoughts which create more harmony,

balance, and well-being within me, and in the world around me.

I automatically, and always, think in a decisive and determined way. I am full of conviction and resolution, and the absolute assurance of the best possible outcome in everything that I do.

I choose to look at the world around me in the bright, healthy light of optimism and self-assurance.

I am satisfied with my self today. I approve of my self and I am content with my being.

I do only those things which are best for me. I create the best within my self, I attract the best in others, and I find the best in the world around me.

I willingly, and without fail, take care of the duties and obligations which I have accepted for my self. I commit only to those responsibilities which I know I can fulfill and which contribute to my well-being and to the well-being of others.

My mind focuses its attention only on those things that I can do something about. If I cannot affect it or direct it—I accept it.

I keep my mind too busy thinking good, healthy, positive, constructive, and productive thoughts to ever have any time for worry, doubt, or uncertainty.

One of the things that I do to eliminate worry from my life is to take action TODAY on those things that require my attention today—and I always look ahead to the bright opportunities of the future.

I control the thoughts I choose. No thought, at any time, can dwell in my mind without my approval or permission.

Every day I create within my self an even greater resolution to live my life free from anxiety and worry—and to give my mind and body the positive benefits of confidence and faith.

CONTROLLING EMOTIONS

Do your emotions ever get in your way? If they do, let me assure you, you are not alone. We were born with the capacity for tremendous emotions—most of them healthy—but we were not automatically given the knowledge of how to deal with some of them. That we had to learn for ourselves.

I have seen people who let their emotions run away with them. Most of us know individuals who constantly get angry for no good reason, strike out emotionally when there is no cause, overreact to fears even when those fears are unfounded, or behave in other ways that cause problems—only because they have not learned to control their own emotions.

There may be times when you *know* it would be better to remain calm, or in control of your self, only to find that your emotions take over. There is a reason why that happens, and there is a remedy.

There is a "cycle" of *situation, thought, chemical response,* and *emotional response* that each of us goes through many times in one day—usually without knowing about it. It works like this:

1. *A situation occurs that could upset you.*

2. *The situation creates thoughts in your mind.*

3. *Your thoughts, in turn, create a physiological—chemical—response in your brain.*

4. *The chemical response that your thoughts initiate creates your emotions, how you feel about the situation.*

5. *Your emotions then create more thoughts of a similar nature, which in turn create another chemical-emotional response, and so on.*

This whole process can take place in no more than a few seconds—or less! Unless you are in control of your original reaction—that is, your *thoughts*—about the situation, your *emotions* take over, and the real control you should have had is taken away from you.

That is why people lose their presence of mind when it would have been far better for them and everyone concerned if they had been able to keep themselves in control. They have not yet learned that part of life is learning to control their emotions.

There are no "bad" emotions. Even such seemingly unnecessary emotions of fear or anger have their proper time and place along with the more positive emotions of joy and love, for example.

However, any emotion left unchecked can cause unnecessary psychological and *physical* stress—in us and in the people around us whom we are affecting.

Don't give in to the old form of self-talk, which might have said, *"That makes me so mad!"; "Why do you try to hurt my feelings?"; "I blow up every time I think about it"; "That really gets to me"; "I just can't handle this"; "I can't control myself"; "I can't deal with my feelings"; "You know what that does to me"; "I don't know what to think anymore"; "I get angry every time I think about it"; "I can't help myself"; "That's just the way I am"; "You'll just have to put up with me"; "You make me so mad"; or "I'm sorry I'm so emotional."*

There is a better way to live—a better way to react and a better way to feel about anything that "happens" to us—and we all know it.

Why do we fight so hard to tell our selves that we are angry, hurt, or unhappy when we could just as easily tell our selves that we are "in control of the situation"? How much better it would be to take control of our reactions—the thoughts that create the emotions in the first place. Most of the other Self-Talk scripts in this book will affect your thoughts—and thereby your emotions—in a positive way. The Self-Talk in the script below can help you keep emotions in control.

I am in control of my thoughts and my emotions. I control them—they do not control me.

I value my self, and I believe that I deserve the best of my self.

Although I make sure that I do those things which expect the best of who I am, I do not need to live my life in a way that allows harmful emotions to get in my way.

I enjoy the deep, strong emotions that I have within me. But I choose to turn those feelings and emotions into forces of good which work for me in my life.

I am understanding and considerate of others, and I do not allow my own emotions to stand in the way of my relationships with others.

I really enjoy dealing with others in a calm, mutually beneficial way.

I have a good personality. I like who I am and I am in control of my *self.*

I am good at being patient with other people and with the realities of life.

When any situation calls for patience, I always keep my self calm, collected, and in control.

I think, act, and live in a way that brings calm and contentment to me and to others around me.

I am healthy, and I do those things which remove unnecessary stress from any area of my life.

I have created in my self the habit of having positive emotions. This habit works for me at all times and in any situation.

I control my emotions easily and naturally.

I have a good attitude about others and a good attitude about my self.

Anytime I am in a situation that in the past could have caused inappropriate emotions, I enjoy the great feeling of being successfully in control.

I am able to be sensitive, warm, and open with people, and I am able to express my feelings in a healthy, positive way.

Because I have a good attitude about my self and my life, I create strong, positive feelings and emotions within me.

Each day I recognize my ability to be in charge of who I am, how I think, and how I feel.

I have learned the skill of creating those emotions that give me peace of mind, improve my physical health, and improve my relationships with those around me—each day, at all times, and in all situations.

I am succeeding in every important area of my life—and even my emotions are a reflection of the winner that I am.

OVERCOMING OBSTACLES

Earlier I recommended some Self-Talk that deals with how you look at problems. The Self-Talk in this script gets even more specific—it tells you about how you personally can overcome the obstacles that present themselves to you.

"Obstacles" are the barriers that stand between you and your objectives. They can be roadblocks to stop you, or they can be nothing more than things to get past to get the job done. How difficult, impossible, or passable your obstacles are is usually up to you.

You alone decide whether you will allow an obstacle to deflate your enthusiasm or undermine your determination to get past it. If you believe that a barrier in your life is impossible to break through, you can be sure it will be. If, on the other hand, you choose to keep going and overcome the obstacle, you probably will do so.

This is one of those Self-Talk scripts which, if you use it frequently and learn to believe it, can help you overcome problems that at one time you would have thought impossible. The words it contains expect a lot from you, but why would you expect anything less?

Try repeating these words to your self when something

difficult stands in your way. Tell your self you *can* overcome it. Say it with emphasis and meaning. Give your self the words, the mental picture, and the belief—and see what happens.

I am a winner! There is no obstacle so great that I cannot overcome it. There is no difficulty so awesome that it stands in my way.

I have strength, absolute determination, and limitless endurance in the pursuit of my goals.

By removing the limitations I have placed on my self in my mind, I have removed many of the barriers which I had only believed to be in front of me—and which, in reality, were never there at all.

I choose to create no problem that does not exist. But I never ignore the problems that are there.

I am practical and realistic. I have absolute confidence in my self to meet and overcome any obstacle in my path.

I always see any barrier to my success in the clear light of understanding. I always meet the challenge with the positive, calm self-assurance of winning!

Each day, when I write my list of things to do, I always add those things which I must do to overcome any obstacle I am facing.

I tackle each problem head on. I decide what I have to do about it, I make the decision to do it, and I get it done.

When I set a goal or determine a task for my self, I believe in the final outcome—right from the start and every step along the way.

I am willing to do any positive thing I have to do to see that what I decide to do gets done—in the most positive possible way.

I have learned that the word "difficult" is more a state of mind than a description of a problem.

Instead of seeing obstacles as "difficult," my mind sees them as just "being there." Not bad. Not impossible. Just there.

I never see barriers as "bad luck" or even "unfortunate." I see them for what they really are. I give them no more and no less importance than they deserve.

Because of my positive, confident attitude about obstacles and difficulties, they are never a source of anxiety or stress for me. I have learned to *deal* with them simply and matter-of-factly— in the most appropriate and expedient way.

When dealing with obstacles and difficulties that are a natural part of any true achievement, I always remember that I have made the decision to *win*. Any obstacle I encounter will give up long before I do.

When you are faced with an obstacle that is especially difficult, listen to a tape of those words, or read them out loud to your self several times in succession. You will be creating a mental, *chemical* response to the words, that could give you just what you need to meet that problem with renewed determination to come out on top.

Then, just before you tackle the problem, reread or listen again to the script entitled "Believing in Incredible You." If you do all that, and if you are absolutely determined to win, I would hate to be the obstacle standing in your way.

CREATING HOPE

How many times has someone thought, "If I can just see light at the other end of the tunnel, I can get through." Without hope, there seems to be no reason to go on. *With* hope, there is every reason to continue.

On the list of the finest human qualities, the word "hope" sits right next to "faith," not far from "belief," and very close to "conviction." That human quality of *hope* may be responsible for more lives saved, more goals reached, more problems solved, and more obstacles overcome than any other quality we know of.

When all else fails, it seems that what we could do with a little *more* of is hope. That is true "spiritually," but it is also true *medically*—physiologically. Medical doctors will tell you that often patients started on the road to recovery when they had hope. Psychologists and psychiatrists will tell you that the turning point—from despair to recovery—with many of their clients or patients happened when those individuals found, or were given, hope.

One of the reasons why people often begin to do better physically or mentally when they *have* hope, is that "hope" inspires "belief." And we have learned that belief is one of the components of the subconscious mind that create chemical changes in the brain. Those chemical responses can be powerful fighters. When it seems that all is lost, we need all the fighters on our team we can get.

That powerful cousin of faith which we call "hope" may play a more important role in our physical and mental well-being than we thought. Having hope creates a new sense of belief, and, in many cases, a new sense of *determination*.

It is that determination that rekindles the fire to *survive*. When we have hope, we give our selves added chemical, physiological, and psychological energy—a vitality to overcome despair and make it through the tunnel to the light beyond.

If you want to create more hope within your self, or if you would like to give the gift of hope to someone else, you can help by creating thoughts that produce the fertile ground from which new belief can grow.

Instead of accepting the despair of futility, create the hope of *possibility*. What you do to create this *hope* could, as it has so often in the past, change the course of what happens next.

I have hope!

I will *not* give up! I know that as long as there is life, *there is hope*.

I refuse to let the problems of life get me down! I know that even the darkest day has a better tomorrow. I expect it, I look for it, and it always comes!

I have *faith*, I have *courage*, and I have *belief*—in my self and in the best possible outcome of any problem I face.

I am strong. And I have the strength I need to see me through!

I look for, and find, the better, brighter side of any problem which comes my way. And I find ways to overcome it.

Instead of allowing my self to live in the dark clouds of despair, I look for the halo of sunlight just behind them.

I accept those things which I cannot change, but I always focus my thoughts on creating the very best outcome of any situation.

I have learned to look at my life, and everything in it, in the broad, clear perspective of understanding. I have learned to say the words "This too shall pass," and trust their truth in my life.

I never give up. I am a winner, and I give my self the energy and the belief to come out on top!

Anytime I am faced with a situation that appears difficult or impossible, I remind my self of the incredible power that hope creates in my mind.

I have patience. I never put off doing what I can, but I am always able to allow the natural, positive forces of my life to work for me.

I keep my spirits up! I think healthy, productive thoughts; I fill my self with the positive energy of believing in the best!

I choose to feel up, think up, act up, and keep my spirits high!

I count my blessings. I am always aware of the many good things which are a part of my life.

I will never give up on life—and life will never give up on me. I have *hope*—and it shows!

Each day I have more hope and more conviction of my ability to overcome any obstacle and defeat any problem.

I have *life, strength, energy, incredible confidence, unbreakable faith*, and an *absolute determination* to win.

OVERCOMING NEGATIVITY IN OTHERS

How *do* you help with—or even get past—the negative programs of someone else? In an earlier chapter in Part I of this book, we discussed this problem. In this section we will look at some of the specific Self-Talk that can help overcome it.

Most of this Self-Talk deals with two things:

> 1. *Helping the other person (with his or her own attitude) when you can and in the best way you can.*

> 2. *Making sure that your own attitude is not adversely affected by someone else.*

Because I work in the field of human behavior, I run into more than my share of people who are at their wits' end because someone they know is so negative that it is making life difficult for both of them.

I've had the opportunity to observe many people, who were willing to try *anything*, finally use their own Self-Talk to help deal with such problems. And I have seen their *Self*-Talk work.

I have never seen a "miraculous" solution to the problem of dealing with another person's negative view of life, but I have seen some remarkable changes take place when the "victim" of another person's negativity stopped *accepting* those negatives!

To accomplish that, you must make a *decision* to do it. Neither you nor I can help someone else look at life more positively when we get caught up in that person's prior, negative programs. If you want to help the other person, or if you just want to avoid the negatives that the other person believes in, first you will have to ensure that your *own* house is in order, that your own attitude is up, willing, and ready.

I'm not sure that I could ever give up on someone. If that someone were a friend or a loved one, I know I could never stop believing that one day that person would recognize his or her real self—and come alive.

When someone moves from being what we call "negative" to being "positive," those watching the change witness an amazing transformation. Seeing someone finally throw out old programs of negative disbelief, and replace them with new programs of positive self-belief, is often compared to watching a caterpillar struggle through its metamorphosis to become a brilliant butterfly.

The difference is, when we see a change take place for the better in the attitudes and in the life of someone we love, it isn't a butterfly on the branch of a tree we are watching, it is the entire future of a human being.

I enjoy showing others the best of themselves. I always accept them at their best.

I am able to recognize positive traits in people that other people often ignore.

I have learned to say the powerful words "I believe in you."

I never expect the impossible from others, but I always expect the best. I let people know that I believe in them and in the many successes that are in store for them.

There is no attitude that defeats me. I am in control of my own thoughts and my own attitudes.

I at no time allow the attitudes of others to affect me in any negative way.

I make sure that my own attitudes serve as a shining example of the positive self-direction of my own life.

People like to be around me, and they can feel the energy I create. I am up, happy, and glad to be alive!

When I sense a negative attitude in someone else, I ignore the negative side and give my energies instead to recognizing that person's most positive traits.

I have learned the benefits of telling my self, "When in doubt, respond in the positive."

I recognize that another person's attitude does not change just because I'd like it to. But I can and do offer belief, encouragement, and confidence in the best possible outcome.

I never, at any time, take responsibility for someone else's attitude. But I do make sure that I take full responsibility for my own.

I know that attitude is a habit that anyone can create, so I choose to create the positive habit of winning in my life.

I make sure that I always deal with any negativity around me in the most worthwhile, positive, and constructive way.

OVERCOMING NEGATIVITY IN YOUR SELF

I have a basic belief in people that as yet has not let me down. It is always best to expect the best of everyone. Although there are times when that doesn't work, for the most part it does.

If you have been having a hard time because you have learned to be too hard on your self, and have gotten into the habit of looking at things "worst first and best last," you should know that everyone has been there with you.

If you are being negative toward your self, you do not have to be. Whatever you have believed about your self, no matter what doubts or misgivings you may have had in the past, you should know that the life within you is special and unique. You are a living expression of the amazing Gift that created all of us.

Trust in this: You were born to be an exceptional human being. You were given the right to live your life to the absolute fullest. And *nothing* should *ever* take that away from you.

When you read the words of Self-Talk below, give your self the chance to know that they are telling you the truth about your self. Someone else who believes in you enough would convince you that they were true. Now it's your turn to do the same for your self.

I have made the decision to see my self and my life in a positive new way.

Now I always look for the best in my self and in everything around me—and the more I look, the more I find.

Anytime I am confronted with any negative thought, I immediately turn the thought around and restate it to my self in the most positive possible way.

I have learned to say to my self, and to others, only those things which reflect positive qualities in my self and in them.

I find new, positive, and worthwhile qualities in my self each day.

I do not allow depression or despair to play any role in my life. I now choose to see my life in the bright, exciting light of opportunities and endless possibilities.

I allow no negativity of any kind, any room or place to live in my life. I would rather be the me that sees my self and my world in a happy, wholesome, positive way.

I enjoy being happy and experiencing the many benefits my positive new attitude creates for me.

I have made the decision to rid my self of any negatives which may have come to me from my past. I am through with them, I no longer need them, and they have no place in my life.

Seeing my self in this new way is important to me. I choose to achieve—and now I know I can!

I associate with positive people. The friends I choose are the friends whose attitudes are Tops!

By spending time with people who are happy, positive, and moving forward in their lives, I become even more enthusiastic for having those same winning qualities myself.

I recognize many good things about my self, my attitude, my today, and my future.

I am now becoming even more of the positive person I was created to be, and I create more winning belief in my self each and every day.

OVERCOMING THE FEAR OF FAILURE

Many *potential* achievements never see the light of day only because people are afraid they *might* fail. I don't know if I have ever met *anyone* who, at one time or another, was not afraid of failing.

Imagine what we might actually accomplish if we *never* feared failure. I would not expect that of anyone, of course, but there are times—too many of them—when it is not the size of the job or the problem that stops us—it is our fear that we might not succeed. What if we *try,* and then *fail?*

I remember the words I first heard as a child, "Trying isn't good enough!" But the truth is, if you allow the possibility of failure to keep you from trying, you have failed before you have even begun.

"Failure" is an attitude based on what you believe about your self. And what you believe is the result of your programming. This means that you can change your attitudes about failure—and begin to look at it differently. When you begin—with new conditioning, new self-directions—to see failure as nothing more than a necessary part of learning and growing, you will start to look at what you do—or *could* do—in a new way.

The choices we face—each of which represents potential "success" or "failure"—often deal with the most normal events of life: A man looks at the telephone and wonders whether he should call a lady he met and ask her out for dinner. A salesperson looks at his prospect list and wonders if the prospective customers on that list will say yes to his presentation or his request for the order. A single parent looks at the household budget she has prepared and begins to think that it just can't work.

Should we go for the chance that we might just succeed, or not? And if we fear *failure*, what should we do? And so, *we may not even attempt the challenge at all.*

Most of our fears about failing are unconscious; we are not even *aware* that we have them. We give our selves every possible excuse why we should *not* do something. We convince our selves that the loan would not go through, or the college would not accept us, or we wouldn't get the job anyway, or that the customer won't buy, or that the budget won't balance. We create reasons that *prove* to us that *it won't work!*

But the *real* reason we stop is because we are *afraid* that if we try, we might *fail*. Most of the Self-Talk in this book will help overcome that single fear—*failure*. It will give you reasons to *try*, and encouragement to go on. The Self-Talk that follows, however, will give you some specific self-directions that confront the fear itself. These self-directions will help you begin to trade in that old attitude that said, "I cannot," for one that says, "Of course I can!"

I believe in my self.

I know that both "failure" and "success" are states of mind—so I keep my mind tuned to success, not failure.

I know that what others call "failure" is nothing more than the opportunity for me to learn, to grow, and to reach my successes.

I am never afraid to *try*.

I know that it is through my willingness to overcome my own past self-doubts that I set the stage for my future achievements.

I enjoy moving forward and staying with it. I never let the fear of failure—of any kind—get in my way.

I never worry about what other people will say about my goals, my attempts at achieving them, or any "failures" I may have along the way.

I do not live my life based on the opinions of others. I make my own decisions and I live them out.

By learning to manage my self, I have given my self the *freedom to fail* and to move on to the successes I create as a result of what I have gained from any failure, or any success.

I do not fear failing. I take responsibility for my actions. I prepare my self with the knowledge and skill that I need to succeed. And I move forward.

I see my self as a "successful" individual. And I know that any failures I may encounter are a necessary part of that success.

I never put off doing something that I know I should do just because I think I might fail. I would rather take *action*, do the best that I can, and know that I had the courage to try.

I accept my failures and I look past them.

I do not live my life dwelling on the failures of my past. I accept them, I learn from them, and I do better today because of them.

I look forward to the many successes which I am now creating for my self. Looking forward and *believing in my self*, is how I choose to live.

Each day I make decisions which affect my self and my life. I never avoid them, I understand their consequences, and I have the faith to see them through.

Even the *word* "failure" has come to mean something different to me now. I have learned that failure is nothing more than a

natural part of life—and a healthy, and essential part of my *success.*

As long as you are willing to try, you will *never* be measured by your failures, *no matter how many of them there may be.* You will be measured only by your successes—and the fact that you were willing to start, stay with it, and finish.

TWENTY-FOUR

SELF-TALK FOR GETTING ORGANIZED AND GETTING THINGS DONE

What fulfillment we could have in our lives if only we had the skill and the inclination to manage the precious commodity called "time." I have so often heard people say, "If only I had more time," or "I just can't seem to get organized." Getting things done, feeling good about it, and having time left over are gifts which only a few of us seem to be able to find. And yet the mastery of time is something most of us could have—if we went about it right.

The Self-Talk in this chapter is about being organized, setting priorities, and managing your time. At the very root of personal organization and the management of time is *Self-Management*—making the choice to take responsibility for your own life. No matter how much of your life seems to be controlled by the time demands of others, you can be sure that taking control of your *self* is one of the most effective ways to take control of your *time*.

Many of the Self-Talk scripts and phrases I have compiled in this book are self-directions that create not only self-esteem but self-*control*—control, by you, of your thoughts, your future, your present, and your *time*. What you do with your thoughts will direct what you do with everything else about you. What you do with your *time* will determine how well you do.

The following Self-Talk is written for those of you who want to have a say in how you end up spending your days. If you would like to have control over more of the moments in your day, you should enjoy the Self-Talk sections on getting more organized and getting more done. I hope they do for you what they have done for others.

GETTING ORGANIZED

There is something especially exhilarating about getting organized. It is a feeling of being on top of things, knowing where you stand, and being in control of at least a part of your life.

Getting organized is a skill. It is a skill that almost anyone can learn; and it is not difficult. But getting organized is also a "frame of mind." All personal organization always starts with an "attitude of organization." That attitude does not come about by luck or by chance; it is created.

If you would like to be more organized, you can be. Most of those who have tackled this skill, and mastered it, will tell you that it is one of the most rewarding accomplishments they have ever achieved.

I am organized and in control of my life. I am in control of myself, my thoughts, my time, my actions, and my future.

I know what to do and when to do it, and I do everything I need to do, when I need to do it.

I program my mind to make the maximum use of my time. I am in control of my time and how to use it. I like being organized, efficient, and on top of things. Controlling my time keeps me that way.

I never waste time—I always "plan" time. And because I plan my time and follow my plan, I always have enough time to do the things I choose to do.

Each day I become more organized and in control of all areas of my life—at home, at work, in my mind and in my thoughts, and in everything that I do.

I am very well organized. Each night I make a list of things I need to do the next day. I set my priorities and I follow them.

I am always on time. I am always right where I need to be, exactly when I need to be there. Being on time is easy for me and the more I control my time and the more organized I become, the easier it is.

I am in control of my feelings, my emotions, my attitudes, and my needs. I control them; they do not control me.

I have the winning vote in the outcome of my own actions. And I choose to live my life by choice, not chance. Therefore, I take the time to take control.

I have an organized and orderly mind. Because I think in an organized way, I conduct my life in an organized manner.

I think in the most positive and productive way at all times and in all things. The way I think is the way I live—and I think "right"!

I am the director of my destiny. I know where I am going and I know why I am going there. My life is in my hands and in my control.

I control my goals and the achievement of my goals. I organize my goals by writing each of them down, along with the steps I need to reach them. One of the reasons for my success is that my goals are clearly defined and organized.

I am in complete control of what I think and how I think. Therefore, I choose to think only those thoughts which help me and which are of genuine benefit to me.

GETTING MORE DONE

Have you ever had times when you said, "I feel like I haven't gotten a single thing done today"? There are people who feel that way about entire years!

If you would like to get more done—and perhaps spend even less time doing it—there is a good chance that you can. Most time-management trainers will tell you that you should be able to get more accomplished, in the same amount of time, just by being aware of what you are doing and learning a new skill or two to help you "organize your accomplishments" a little more carefully.

To get the best *out* of your self, however, it will help if you first feed the best *in*to your self. Regardless of how much you have gotten (or not gotten) done in the past, there is an excellent chance that changing your Self-Talk could create some exciting and worthwhile changes in how much you are able to get done—if you put your *mind* to it, *without* spending any more time doing it.

I achieve more because I do more. I enjoy giving extra effort and getting extra results.

I am organized and efficient. I have mastered the skill of getting more done in less time.

I approach each task with the determination to find and follow the most productive and most efficient means of completing it.

I work hard, but I also work smart. I plan my activities carefully and I carefully follow my plan.

I am aware of the time I spend doing anything that I do.

I avoid doing those things which waste time, and I enjoy spending my time doing those which are the most beneficial and worthwhile.

My accomplishment is above average because I am above average. I expect more from my self and that's what I get.

I place great value on taking action. I see what needs to be done and I do it.

I accomplish more by increasing the amount of effort and time I put into the things I do.

Both the quality and the quantity of what I do are important to me. And the rewards I achieve are well worth the investment I make.

I increase my output by concentrating my energy and focusing my attention on the job at hand. When it comes to getting something done, I have a "one-track mind."

I enjoy working hard and I enjoy the benefits which my work produces—and the satisfaction of achievement which comes to me.

The more energy I put into the task, the better the job I do, and the greater is my reward. And earning a greater reward creates extra energy in me.

I like the satisfaction of knowing that I work hard and I do anything I do well. I look forward each day to increasing my effectiveness and accomplishing even more.

I have a good attitude about the work I do. I know that I get out of it what I put into it, and I make sure that I always go the extra mile to get the job done right.

STOPPING PROCRASTINATION

If procrastination, putting things off, is a problem for you, you are not alone. Procrastination is one problem that many people would like to conquer. And because procrastination is a habit, it *can* be conquered.

To overcome this habit takes as much determination as it takes practice; nothing helps conquer procrastination as much as an irrevocable *decision* to overcome it.

We have all seen the effects of putting things off. History shows that wars have been fought, fortunes have been lost, and lives have been ruined, all because people did not do what they knew they should do when they needed to do it.

In your own life you have undoubtedly experienced the results of not doing something you knew you should do— only to learn that the consequences were far more painful than doing the task itself would have been in the first place.

One woman told me that she eventually lost her marriage because she could not bring herself to balance the checkbook. A promising student I met admitted that he fell behind in college, not because he was not smart enough to pass the tests, but because he turned in most of his assignments late. He had completed the assignments, and they would have earned him A+ grades if he had turned them in on time. At a seminar I gave to a group of business executives, one manager told me he could increase his company's sales by 30 or 40 percent if he could find a way to teach his salespeople to do the follow-up work on their accounts when it *should* be done!

The problem of procrastination has never been very selective—it is a problem which, from time to time, has plagued most of us. And yet when addressed, it is a problem that is *not* difficult to overcome. It is a problem that is almost entirely surmountable when we learn, and practice, a few basic principles of Self-Management.

Those principles are included in the Self-Talk below. Along with some of the other Self-Talk scripts that make up this chapter, conquering procrastination should not prove to be impossible. It could, however, prove to be one of the most *worthwhile* goals you have ever set for your self.

I always do everything I need to do—when I need to do it.

I enjoy getting things done—on time or before and in just the right way. Instead of putting things off, I get things done. And I enjoy the feeling of accomplishment and satisfaction that this gives me.

I accept only those responsibilities which I will live up to. I agree to do only those things that I WILL do. With me, an agreement made is an agreement kept.

Because I organize my time and my self, I *make* time and *take* time to meet my obligations—and I complete every task I set for my self.

I never allow indecision to make my choices for me. Because I make decisions rapidly and with conviction—and because I act on my decisions—procrastination plays no role in my accomplishments.

I always look for ways that I *can* get something done instead of finding reasons why I can't.

My mind is organized and so is my time. I am a winner. And I value the time I have to accomplish the many things I want to do. Time is a valuable tool which I appreciate, respect, and put to very good use.

Each night, before I retire, I make a simple list of the things I am going to do the following day. I list each item in order of its importance to me. This keeps me organized and in control. And it gives me a daily plan to follow.

I turn hesitation into determination. I turn indecision into action. And I replace procrastination with the completion of a job well done.

I immediately turn any thought which could lead to putting something off—into a thought that leads to ACTION. In this way I always stop procrastination—procrastination never stops me!

I choose to avoid falling into the trap of being too busy to get things done. I make my list, I confidently follow it—and I have the willpower to stay with it.

I take the time to plan my time. By following the schedule that I set for my self each day, I have learned to turn wasted time into busy, productive "winning time."

Getting started is never a problem for me. Because I take

positive action, do it now, and get it done, I accomplish more than ever before—and still have time left over!

I have learned to recognize my time wasters and now I avoid *them* instead of avoiding the things I need to do to get the job done.

SETTING PRIORITIES AND MANAGING TIME

The effective use of personal, individual time has been the subject of numerous books, and a multitude of management seminars. Your *time* is one of the three most natural resources you have to offer. (The other two are your *energy* and your *mind*.) How you use your time will affect or determine how successful you are at almost anything.

Managing time is actually the management of your priorities. If you work on and develop every other personal goal this book has touched on, the end result will still ultimately depend on the *priorities* you set.

If you use your time well, you will achieve more of the goals you set for yourself. If you do everything else right, but fail to recognize the importance of the fleeting moments that make up your life, you will fall short of the final goal of living your life at its top potential.

What do your past programs on managing time and the priorities in your life look like? What have you been saying to your self—consciously and unconsciously—about how you spend your time?

Some of the self-talk that I have overheard people using will *never* help *anyone* manage time well. Among the many frequently used self-talk statements I have collected over the years, some of the most self-crippling are: *"I never have enough time"; "I don't know where the day went"; "I wish I had more time"; "I just don't have the time"; "They just don't make enough hours in a day"; "I would do it if I had the time"; "I have more to do than I can possibly get done"; "Sometimes I don't know what to do first"; "I'll get to it when I have the time";* or that classic statement *"Where did all the time go?"*

Self-Management, in the final analysis, is a means of managing each of our natural resources in the best possible way. How you manage your own precious time on earth will ultimately determine how well you did while you were here.

I am in control of my self and my life. I know what is important to me and what is not.

First Things First is one motto which I live by.

Because I take full responsibility for my self and for my life, I never leave my priorities to chance or up to someone else.

I recognize the importance of taking control of my time and my priorities.

I write my list of things to do each day, and I always arrange the items on the list in order of their importance to me.

I manage my thoughts well, and I take time to exercise good judgment in everything that I do.

I keep my life in balance. I know that "in balance" is "in control"—and I keep it that way.

I consciously choose my priorities, how I spend my time, and how I live my life—from major events to the smallest details.

I understand the order of importance in all things that I do—both large and small.

I always do what is truly best for me at all times and in all circumstances. I am always mindful of my true priorities and I follow them.

An accurate description of me would include the words "sensible," "level-headed," "discriminating," "well rounded," "practical," "well balanced," and "in control."

Because I set my own priorities and I know the importance of each thing that I do, I give it exactly the amount of time and attention it deserves.

I have no habits which control me or allow any part of my life to be out of balance in any way.

I have balance in all areas of my life—my work, my home life, family, friends, hobbies, eating, sleeping, exercising, improving my self. I maintain a healthy balance in everything I do.

I take the time to think about how I actually spend my time. And I make sure that I spend my time doing those things which are of the greatest possible value to me.

I live every day of my life in a composed, orderly, and self-controlled way.

With me, moderation, common sense, discrimination, and balance are a way of life.

I am always aware of the consequences of anything that I do. Therefore, I always do only those things which I know will result in the consequences which I want to take place in my life.

I never let anything get out of line, out of balance, or out of control. In my life everything has its proper time, its proper place, and its proper priority.

As I read or listen to these words and visualize their meaning in my mind, I am more aware than ever before of the importance of my time and of the priorities which I set for my self each day.

Each day I perfect my priorities and create even more "winning time" in my life.

You will always be the only *true* owner of your time. Other people will try to control your time for you, but it is not their right. Instead of living one day of your life believing that "you don't have the time," try spending one day telling your self that you *do* have the time—to do with exactly what *you* choose. Of course, you will have obligations to meet. And because you are a good Self-Manager, you will meet them.

But what about the *rest* of the time? The busiest, most successful people I know somehow have time left over to do whatever they want to do. Their secret is that they manage their time well. It is not a gift. It is not good luck or fortune. It is an attitude and a skill. With practice, you can create the attitude. The right attitude will produce the skill.

SPECIAL SELF-TALK FOR SUCCESSFUL LIVING

As we approach the end of this journey to Self-Management together, there are a few more thoughts and self-directions which I must share with you. They are some of the most important "self-beliefs" I have ever learned.

The words of Self-Talk in this chapter tie together all the other words of Self-Talk. They give them resonance—and a final important purpose. Anyone can learn self-directions and benefit from using them. But tying those self-directions to your personal goal of becoming a truly unique and special individual makes all of the previous words of Self-Talk far more worthy of attention and practice.

Learn the kind of Self-Talk that gets you to solve problems, think clearly, defeat depression, change your habits, become healthier, take responsibility, make decisions, improve your marriage or your personal relationships. Read them, listen to them on tape, or write your own. They can help you direct your thoughts in a simple, productive, and worthwhile way, and you will see their effects in many areas of your life.

But there is one more step you must take to put the *rest* of your Self-Talk to work. It concerns the words that create within you an *environment* of "living successfully."

To do that, it is necessary to recognize that you *deserve* to succeed, that you make the decision to take control of your life, that you have the *faith* to see it through, that you learn to create the final picture of the best of your self, and that you begin *today* to carry out the obligation to reach more of the potential that you were born to fulfill.

DESERVING TO "SUCCEED"

If you have ever thought that it was not your lot in life to "succeed," then stop for a moment and listen to the voice inside you that tells you it is your *right* to succeed. That voice speaks the truth. It has been your *right*, from the moment of your birth, to attain any height of human potential you choose. That is true of everyone, and that is true of *you*.

There is no such thing at the moment of birth as a "lesser" person or a "greater" person. Those descriptions of human potential—or the lack of it—are attached to us without any regard for the *truth* of who as *individuals* we really are.

Each of us comes into this world with profound potential. We either live up to it, or we do not. And in most cases it is up to us and up to what we have come to accept and believe about our selves to realize it.

If you believe that you have a natural right to live life to the best of your ability, then you will do better at almost everything you do. But if you have learned to believe that having success in life is the right of others but not *yours*, then you were misled.

You have *every right* to succeed in your life. Don't ever let anyone else (or your self) tell you that you do not!

If you and I were to meet and talk, even for a short while, I would show you facets of your self that would amaze you. I would not have to create them. They would be parts of you that have been there all the time.

When I say the words "You are incredible," on one of my tapes, I am not speaking to some mythical person. I know that those words are true—and they are a description of you.

Get rid of any doubts you might have about who you *are* or who you *were*. Get rid of, forever, any uncertainty you might have about whether you are "lucky," "unlucky," "destined to succeed," "destined to be average," or *destined* to be anything other than the incredibly happy and successful person you were born to be.

Achievement is your birthright. It is in your genes. Every human being is born to survive, grow (mentally, physically, and spiritually), and achieve his or her best potential. For whatever reason—survival of the species or spiritual growth—everyone was born to "progress." That is a biological fact.

I relate this to you so you know that your desire to be *better*—is *natural*. That is the way you and I were made. There aren't any exceptions. Every one of us, without exception, was designed *biologically* to *succeed*.

Do you deserve to achieve? Of course you do! *Your potential is a natural expectation of your birth!*

Can you imagine how many good, potentially capable individuals there are living on this earth right now who believe that they *cannot* succeed or do not *deserve* to have the best of what life offers?

Deserving to succeed is one of those gifts that life has given us. It only seems right that we should accept it.

After the release of my book *What to Say When You Talk to Your Self,* I was asked by many of my readers to write the script for a new cassette tape of Self-Talk on "deserving." So for those who asked, and for you, these are the words I wrote.

I deserve to succeed in my life.

My successes are the result of how I think and what I do—and I have learned to *think* those things, and *do* those things that *work!*

I enjoy being *me!* I like the things that I do "well" and I like the things I do "well enough." Because I accept my self, I never expect perfection of my self—I only expect the best of who I am.

I have the ability to make choices in my life—and I make them! Therefore, I deserve the results that my choices create.

In my life I am not a victim—I am an achiever.

I deserve to live my life to the fullest. I know that what I get out of it is up to what I put into it.

I also deserve to recognize the opportunities which life presents to me. When I meet an opportunity, I assess what to do about it, work hard, persevere, achieve, and enjoy the results.

I am a person of quality and strength. And my success is the result of who I am and how I think.

I am entitled to the fulfillment of my self—in every area of my life. It is my rightful heritage as a worthy human being.

Each day I earn the right to succeed. I create, work for, and earn each and every one of my successes.

The more I realize that *I deserve,* the truer it becomes.

I have learned to accept the positive results that come from managing my self.

I also accept the successes which I work to create. I am thankful for each of them, and I willingly accept the joy and the blessings they bring to my life.

I was not created to fail; I was created to *succeed.* Success is a part of who I am and a part of *everything* about me.

I was designed and created, in body and mind, *to achieve!* My success is not only my reward; success is my *responsibility.*

Each day I recognize and accept my worth as an individual, and my right to succeed. I am living my life in a way that creates harmony, well-being, peace of mind, and every other facet of success—and I deserve it!

TAKING CONTROL OF YOUR LIFE

There is no potion you can take that will automatically put your life in order for you. Nor is there someone *else* who can do it for you. Taking control of your life will always, ultimately be up to you.

I have never believed that taking control of one's own life is an easy task. It is certainly something that is easier said than done. But I do believe that taking over the reins of your self, your goals, your choices, your activities is one of the most important tasks you can ever undertake.

Since the alternative is to let the random chances of life, or the whims of others, control *your* happiness, *your* success, *your* peace of mind—learning to take that control for your self is certainly a better choice.

You have come far. By now you may even be getting a twinge or two of the feeling that says, "Let's get on with it! Let's get moving. It's time." If you have made the decision to be in control of your life, then it is time to do it.

Life is becoming truly exciting for me. I am learning the joy of taking control of my own life!

I have decided to let go of those things which I had allowed to stop me or hold me back in the past.

I now concentrate on those things which help me take hold of my self, focus my efforts, and direct my self in an exciting new way.

I may have been good before—but I'm even *better* now!

I take the time to determine what I want from my life. Now I know what I want and where I am going.

I never feel that I am a victim of the circumstances of my own life. I do not live my life by accident, but by my choice and my design.

I have the strongest voice in determining the direction of my own future.

I enjoy making the decisions that affect my life. Making those decisions and acting on them gives me confidence and determination to reach my goals.

I take control of all parts of my life. I take care of even the smallest details that affect my happiness and success in any way.

I never put things off, so I get things done! Because I am taking control of my self, I make sure that I am in control of all of my responsibilities.

I have learned to replace the words "That's life, and there is nothing I can do about it" with the words "That's my *choice*— and there *is* something I can do about it!"

I now control my time and my activities. I know what my objectives are. I do everything I need to do to reach them. And I make progress every single day.

I enjoy getting my life in order. I now have more peace of mind than ever before.

I am proud of my self for taking the time to take control.

I have replaced uncertainty with solid new self-directions. I have replaced doubt with self-assurance. And I have replaced any misgivings about myself with a bright new picture of *who I am*, and how I *choose* to be.

I no longer accept any negative conditioning or directions from my self, from anyone else, or from the world around me.

I enjoy the feeling I get when I take a stand, dig in, and refuse to accept anything less than I bargained for.

By taking control of my life I not only control my thoughts, my actions, and my direction—I also control and conquer any unnecessary limitations I had placed on my self in the past.

I have learned the "truth" about my self, and I like what I have learned. I now know that I am capable of doing *anything* I choose to do. And *I* choose to be in control of *me*.

What a wonderful way to feel about your self. What a wonderful way to *live!* If you have decided that *that* is the way you would like to live, at least more of the time, then let me give you some encouragement.

I have seen people who literally amazed themselves once they decided to get their lives "in control." I have seen people lift from themselves huge burdens which they had carried on their shoulders for years—never believing that they would ever be rid of them. Many of them did not believe, until they tried, that they could do it. Many of their closest friends and loved ones did not think they could do it either.

I encourage you to prove that your old doubts about your self were wrong! The *truth* is, if you really want to put your self in control of your life, you *can*. Doing that takes a lot of courage, and a lot of determination to stay with it. And it takes one more thing: *"faith."*

HAVING "FAITH"

Having "faith" is not an accident. We have it when we demand it of our selves. We can need it, practice it, and pray for more of it, but it is up to each of us at least to *help* create it. Books, sermons, lectures, and theses have been written entirely on the subject of faith. *Without* faith, we falter, and our successes are somehow less, our victories shallow. *With* faith our minds prosper, and so do the works that follow.

I have never known of a single great mind, the finest individual, who did not attribute his or her achievement, at least in part, to that elusive power we call "faith." This power cannot be bought in a store or measured in a laboratory. And yet the *results* of "having faith" can be measured in anything that we do.

Having faith allows us to have *belief* in our selves, belief in the best of our ideals, belief in our dreams, belief in anything we do, and belief in the best of the people around us.

If I had to summarize, in one word, a combination of

trust, belief, assurance, dependence, confidence, hope, reliance, certainty, and expectation,—the one word that ties them all together would be "faith." It is when we add faith to our dreams that they are nourished and come to life.

I once thought that having "faith" was a gift that belonged only to those fortunate enough to possess it. But the truth is that *anyone* can have more of it. You can do more than listen to the words of wisdom from someone in your church or anyone else who tells you to *"have faith."* They are giving you good advice. But there is something that *you* can *do* about it: The more faith you *demand* of your self, the more you will have.

Go ahead! Have more faith. No matter where you are, where you have been, or who you are now, faith will give you more of the spiritual (and physiological) energy that is a part of every worthwhile goal you have.

Talk to your self. Give your self *faith*. Don't let up; insist on it. Demand it! Practice it! And then watch the results that faith creates.

I have faith.

Each day I become even stronger in my faith and in the outcome of my own future.

My faith lives in every part of my life. It is always there and always with me, creating even more strength, confidence, and belief within me.

I am conscious of the role that my faith plays in my life—and its importance to my total well-being.

Each day I give my self the conscious direction to openly receive the spiritual strength which comes to me.

I never rely on anyone else to create my faith for me.

I am aware of the powerful consequences of my own thoughts, and the role that they play in my life.

I take full responsibility for my thoughts. I use the capability of my mind in the best possible way.

I direct the resources of the miracle of my own mind to work for me for the betterment of my life and the lives of others.

I allow no thought that is harmful to me to dwell in my mind at any time.

I choose to think *only* those thoughts which increase my faith and create even more winning belief in my life!

The life I live is the expression of my faith. And each day I live to express that faith in many wonderful ways.

Each day I create wellness and goodness in every area of my life.

My faith is strong and never fails me. And I am determined to live each day in a way that creates even more faith and enthusiasm within me.

I have faith.

BECOMING THE TOTAL PERSON

There is so much we can *be,* if only we would give our selves the chance. There is more to any of us than ever sees the light of day. You, right now, have more capability, more potential within you—as you are today—than you have ever known. Imagine how you might feel if you were given a vision in which you had a crystal-clear picture of your self living up to your finest expectations—living out the marvelous reality of who you *really* are.

That vision is not a dream. That picture of you is as real, and as touchable, as the picture you have of your self today. But it is a picture that is somehow better, more secure, happier, more fulfilled, more *complete.*

It is a wonderful picture to imagine about our selves. It points the way, quietly prodding, suggesting, and encouraging us to proceed. We may never become as enlightened as we *could* be, but we can get closer to our real selves than we could have if we hadn't tried.

The Self-Talk in this script opens the door to seeing your

self in a very special way. It is the kind of Self-Talk that allows you to see your self from a wider perspective; it gives you a glimpse, a small vision, of who you might *really* be.

This Self-Talk gives each of us a portrait of *who we are at our best;* it helps us recognize some of the highest ideals we strive for.

I am in touch with who I really am. I am involved with the creation of my own destiny. I am in control of my life, in control of my self, and in control of the direction of my own future.

There is an abundance of healthiness and wellness in all areas of my life. I am strong and healthy in mind, body, and spirit.

I find value in my life and in all things in it.

Life is a beautiful place to be, and there is richness in all aspects of my being.

Life is the classroom for my soul. Here I learn many wonderful things. I am a good student in life, and I learn my lessons well.

I have opened my mind to the treasures of my life, and they come to me in great abundance.

I have a true sense of who I am and where I am going. I have taken a firm hand in the outcome of my own destiny.

I believe in greatness. I believe that it is mine. I am creating it and I am living it.

I find fulfillment in some area of my life each day. I live fully and completely. Life is richly rewarding to me.

I live my entire life by the choices I make. I am the master of all my thoughts and of all my actions. I am the master of my self.

I create completeness in every part of my self. And each of the

individual parts work together to create unity and wholeness in my life.

I am an exceptional human being. I was intended to be, and I AM. I am special to others around me, and I am special to myself.

I constantly strive to strengthen and improve any area of my self that seeks further growth and advancement—keeping all areas of my life in balance and in harmony with each other.

I am creating the me that I see in my mind. Though I have very far to go, I am pleased with the me that I am today. And I am only just now beginning.

If you have not already done so, make the decision never to spend one *moment* more agonizing over what you are *not*. Tell your self instead what you *are*, and what you *can be*, using the best words of self-belief. The directions you give to your self are valuable, and it makes no sense to waste even one of them. You deserve to get the optimum from the person that is you.

That *life*, that "soul," that unique person that is *you*, was *created* to *succeed*, to achieve, to learn, to grow, and to become the optimum you can possibly be. Why would it be otherwise?

Reaching for your highest expectations is a worthy goal—certainly one of the worthiest you could ever have. I encourage you to *expect to become* the best of your self— and *never* to let up.

LIVING TODAY, *TODAY*

And so we come to the final script (for now) that will bring to a close this session of Self-Talk. If you were writing the final script, what would you say? What *could* you say, in Self-Talk, that has not already been said?

There is actually much more that we can say to our selves that we have not said in this book. There are details, individual problems, personal goals, and specific objectives that could benefit from some good Self-Talk. But we have made a start.

The purpose of the Self-Talk in these pages has been just that: to help you make a start. It was not intended to solve every problem, or support every change you might choose to make. If it has gotten you to think about your *own* Self-Talk, and what you might want to say to your self in the future, then it has done its job.

For me, the last script has never really been the last; it is one of those Self-Talk scripts I keep going back to. It is the kind of Self-Talk that takes self-direction one important step further: It asks *questions,* and it comes up with the right kind of answers.

I suspect that if more of us used this kind of Self-Talk every day, *most* of our lives would be better.

I have given the cassette version of this Self-Talk to my closest friends as my "very best" gift to them. I have given a copy of that same tape to children, my college-age son, corporate presidents, teachers and even my parents. It is a Self-Talk cassette that *anyone* can get a lift from.

This is the script that talks to you about today, *today!* It is the "now" kind of Self-Talk that puts today—and tomorrow—in focus. A few years ago, when I was first studying and writing Self-Talk, before Self-Talk scripts or prerecorded Self-Talk cassettes were readily available, I was writing about the idea of each of us having a "personal coach," a *best friend* at our side, every day, to give us the words of encouragement and motivation that we so often need.

I had often wished that Self-Talk "coach" were at *my* side when I needed him. I did not expect someone to hold a silver spoon of Self-Talk to my mouth every moment of the day—but there were times when a little encouragement would have helped.

The script below differs slightly from the others in that it speaks to you both in the first person and in the third person—it speaks to you from an *outside* you, and to you from an *inside* you, in the same script.

This is the kind of Self-Talk that experienced Self-Talkers use. It represents the next level of programming—the kind of Self-Talk that happens almost automatically after you have been practicing Self-Talk for a while. Try it out. You may like the way it talks to you—and gets you to answer back!

I hope that you will take the following Self-Talk to heart, as I have, for as long as you choose to live *this* day—and *tomorrow* and the *next* day—as *the most important days you will ever live*.

"Hello! How are you today?"
I'm doing just great! I like my self, I like what I'm doing in my life, and I'm glad to be alive!

"How do you feel about today?"
Today is a good day. I've set my goals, I know what to do, and I'm ready to do it.

"Do you know why this day is important to you?"
Yes, I do! Today is *today!* This is the only chance I will ever have to make today the best day of my life. So I've decided to make today the best day I've ever had.

"What will you tell your self about today that will help you make it special?"
Today is a day for living. Today is the day that I find the joy in my life. Today is the day when I make things work. And *today* is the day that I will get things *done!*

"How do you feel about your past *today?"*
I respect and appreciate the lessons I have learned from my past, but I have left the limitations of my past behind. I see today as an incredible opportunity to live *today*—and build a better future in front of me.

"Will you learn anything new *today?"*
I learn something new every day. Each day I live is a day I learn. Today especially! Today is a good day for me to learn something new.

"What will you do if you have a problem?"
I already know that most problems aren't really problems at all. Today I will see problems as nothing more than situations that I can handle. I'm good at dealing with problems, and I don't mind them at all!

"Won't this be just another average *day for you, as it would be for anyone else?"*
No day is an "average" day for me. I make every day count. And that means that I will find a way to make *today* count!

"Are you sure you're 'up to' making today something special?"
I keep my self up. I know that every day that I live is only as good as I make it. I am up to it, I look forward to it, and I'm doing it!

"How do you feel? *How is your energy today?"*
I feel *great!* My energy is high, I take care of my self, I'm in good shape, and I'm living at my best!

"How is your life?"
My life is good. I know who I am, I know where I am going, and I know what I have to do. I take care of my responsibilities, and I take care of my future. I'm glad to be here, and my life is better for me now than it has ever been before.

"Do you get enough rest and recreation?"
I make sure that I get the rest I need and I always *re*-create my energies in healthy, wholesome ways. I exercise, I rest, I sleep, I plan, I take time off, and I enjoy my work.

"How are you getting along with the people around you today?"
I work at making my relationships work. I practice listening, understanding, being supportive, and being the best of my self. I care about other people and other people care about me.

"How do you feel about your future *today?"*
My future looks bright. I plan for it, I prepare for it, and I believe in the best for it. But I make sure that I do what I need to do *today*—so that I will have a good future when I get there.

"Do you have any other directions you would like to give your self for today?"
I always give my self extra directions to help me make the best of every day. These are just a few to get me started, and I'll add some others throughout the day. I will tell my self things like:

Today is important to me.

I live in the "now." I plan for the future, and every day in front of me, but today I will do my best for today.

Every minute of today will count for me.

"Are you happy?"
I am happy. I am living my life in worthwhile ways. I like myself, I like my goals, I like my achievements, and I am moving forward in my life.

"You are an exceptional human being. I know that today will go well for you."

I have listened many times to that Self-Talk script, and it has never failed to change my day for the better. Why does it work? Because it uses the best of the brain and the mind to prepare us for the creation of success—one day at a time.

That is the nature of any good Self-Talk. It does its job, whether it is written, recorded, spoken, or remembered, one day at a time.

Self-Talk prepares us for the creation of success. That is what it was intended to do. And that is what it does.

E·P·I·L·O·G·U·E

Those are just a few Self-Talk words. We can read them, think them, write them down, listen to them, and perhaps will even act on some of them. But most of our real words of Self-Talk will never be written down, nor will we ever hear them spoken. They will be spoken quietly, without our ever knowing it, to our selves.

If we could only hear the words we use, inside our selves, when we talk to our selves, if we could see them written down, I suspect that what we would hear or read would surprise us. If we could read a computer program of our own thoughts—the nudges and tugs, the questions and self-doubts, all the fears and worn-out old beliefs—we would be amazed at what we would find.

But we will never see most of our programming. We will never know how much of it is making us stop, when we should go on, how much of it is telling us what we cannot do, when if we had believed only a little differently, we could have done it. We will never see the thoughts that make us ill or create unhealthiness in our lives. We will not see a computer printout of our imagined inadequacies. We will not, like old Sartebus in the story, take an inventory of the limitations we carry with us.

So we are not always sure what *really* needs changing within us; we don't always know what to get rid of and what not to. Some of our old programming is obvious; most of it is not.

How, then, do we know what to change? How do we know which is the *right* Self-Talk to use so that our better programming of today will safely replace the programming of the past that gave us less?

Even though the mind of man is finally figuring out the mind of man, we have not yet learned how to read everything that is in it. We can only listen to what we have been saying to our selves, and know that what we are hearing is only the smallest part of what we are actually saying to our selves inside. Even the best researchers do not know what we *could* do with our minds if we learned how best to use them.

But what we *do* know is that if we want to learn, grow, or change, the mind will help us. The incredible organ we call a brain will, if asked, do more for us than most people have ever asked it to do. We are capable of so much more than most of us ever become. We live in the shadow of our old selves, expecting and accepting less than we could have achieved had we given our selves a chance.

LIVE OUT THE TREASURES OF YOUR SELF

Now it's *your* turn. We haven't learned everything yet, but we have found a few answers to some questions. We have learned that if we want to change our lives in some small or important way, we know what we must do. If we want more self-esteem, we know, at least in part, where to get it. If we want more determination, we know what to do about that. If we want to take more responsibility for our selves, we know where to start doing it. If we want to have more control over our own lives, we can have it.

So why don't we *change* a few things, set a few things *right? Let's stand up, speak for our selves, refuse to accept the inevitable, and get a grip on our destinies!*

No matter who you are right now, whatever you thought you were and wherever you were led in the past, just imagine where, by your own choice and your own self-belief, you could lead your *self—now*. What will you say to your self the rest of today? What will you tell your self about you tomorrow morning? And what will you tell your self about *you* the next day, and the next?

Will you tell your self the best about you, or will you tell your self something less? If we met at some time in your future, I would know what you had decided to do. Both of us would see the results of that one small decision, in every part of your life. Never sell your self short. Find the treasures in your self, and live them out.

You can be sure that there is more to you than what you have seen so far. The best parts of your self deserve to be lived to their fullest. *If you were not born to live out the treasures of your self, you would not have been given them in the first place.*

Your treasure is waiting. Enjoy it.